THE CREATION OF THE WORLD
AND OTHER BUSINESS

The Creation of the World
and Other Business

A Play

ARTHUR MILLER

The Viking Press / New York

For Inge

THE CREATION OF THE WORLD
AND OTHER BUSINESS

CHARACTERS

GOD

ADAM

EVE

LUCIFER

ANGELS:

   RAPHAEL

   AZRAEL

   CHEMUEL

CAIN

ABEL

Act I

Music.
A night sky full of stars. Day spreads its pristine light, form-
ing shadows in the contrasting sunlight. It is Paradise, the
ultimate Garden—which is to say that it is all an impression
of color rather than terrestrial details of plants and vines.
Only one such feature stands apart; from the left, reaching
out like an inverted, finger-spread hand, is a tree branch with
golden leaves, from which hangs—an apple.

God appears on his throne above the acting level. He is
deep in thought as he tries to visualize the inevitable future.

Now, as light spreads, the caw of a crow sounds, the
dawn-welcoming chatter of monkeys, the hee-hawing ass,
the lion's echoing roar, seals barking, pigs grunting, the
loon's sudden laughter—all at once in free cacophony.

And as they subside and day is full, one of the shadows
moves—a man, Adam, who reaches up above his head and
plucks a fig and, propped up against a rock, crosses his legs
and idly chews. He is in every way a man and naked, but
his skin is imprinted with striped and speckled shadows,
an animated congealment of light and color and darkness.

God emerges behind and to one side of him. He looks
about, at the weather, up at the sky. Then He turns and
looks down at Adam, who gradually feels His presence,
and with only the slightest start of surprise. . . .

ADAM: Oh! Good morning, God!

GOD: Good morning, Adam. Beautiful day.

ADAM: Oh, perfect, Lord. But they all are.

GOD: I've turned up the breeze a little. . . .

ADAM: I just noticed that. *Holds up a hand to feel it.* This is exactly right now. Thanks, Lord.

GOD: I'm very pleased with the way you keep the garden. I see you've pruned the peach tree.

ADAM: I had to, Lord. An injured branch was crying all night. Are we going to name more things today?

GOD: I have something else to discuss with you this morning, but I don't see why we couldn't name a few things first. *He points.* What would you call that?

ADAM: That? I'd call that a lion.

GOD: Lion. Well, that sounds all right. And that?

ADAM: That? Ahhh . . . lamb?

GOD, *trying the word*: Lamb.

ADAM: I don't know what it is today—everything seems to start with L.

GOD: I must say that *looks* like a lamb. And that?

ADAM: L, L, L . . . That should be—ah . . . labbit?

GOD, *cocking His head doubtfully*: Labbit doesn't seem—

ADAM, *quickly*: You're right, that's wrong. See, I was rushing.

GOD: Slow down, we have all the time in the world.

ADAM: Actually, that looks like something that should begin with an R. . . . Rabbit!

GOD: Rabbit sounds much better.

ADAM, *happily*: Rabbit, rabbit!—oh, sure, that's much better.

GOD: How about that?

ADAM: I've been wondering about that. I have a feeling it should have a name that goes up and down, like . . . ka . . . ka . . .

GOD: Yes? Go on. . . . *Ka* what?

ADAM, *undulantly*: Ca-ter-pill-ar.

GOD: What an amazing creature you've turned out to be; I would never have thought of "Caterpillar" in a million years. That'll be enough for today. I imagine you've noticed by this time that all the animals live in pairs—there are male and female?

ADAM: I'm so glad you mentioned that.

GOD: Oh, it disturbs you?

ADAM: Oh no, Lord, nothing disturbs me.

GOD: I'm glad to see that you've settled for perfection.

ADAM: It just seemed odd that, of all the creatures, only I am alone. But I'm sure you have your reasons.

GOD: Actually, Adam—and I know this won't shake your confidence—but now and then I do something and, quite frankly, it's only afterwards that I discover the reasons. Which, of course, is just as well. In your case it was extremely experimental. I had just finished the chimpanzee and had some clay left over. And I—well, just played around with it, and by golly there you were, the spitting image of me. In fact, that is probably why I feel such a special closeness to you: you sprang out of my instinct rather than some design. And that is probably why it never occurred to me to give you a wife, you see.

ADAM: Oh, I see. What would it look like? Or don't you know yet?

GOD: Supposing I improvise something and see how it strikes you.

ADAM: All right. But would I have to—like, talk to it all the time?

GOD: What in the world gave you an idea like that?

ADAM: Well, these lions and monkeys and mice—they're all constantly talking to each other. And I so enjoy lying on my back and just listening to the lilacs budding.

GOD: You mean you'd rather remain alone?

ADAM: I don't know! I've never had anybody.

GOD: Well, neither have I, so I'm afraid I can't help you there. Why don't we just try it and see what happens?

ADAM: Of course, Lord, anything you say.

GOD: Lie down, then, and I'll put you to sleep.

ADAM: Yes, Lord.

He lies down. God feels his rib cage.

GOD: I'll take out a bottom rib. This one here. You'll never know the difference.

ADAM, *starting up*: Is that—fairly definite?

GOD: Oh, don't worry, I shouldn't have put it in in the first place, but I wanted to be extra sure. Now close your eyes.

ADAM, *lying back nervously*: Yes, sir. . . . *Starts up again.* Is this also going to be experimental, or—I mean how long are we going to keep her?

GOD: Now look, son, you don't have to hang around her every minute. If it gets too much, you just walk off by yourself.

ADAM: Oh, good. *Starts lying down, then sits up nervously.* I just wondered.

GOD: Sleep, Adam! *He ceremonially lowers his hands on Adam's rib. Something stirs on the periphery, rising from the ground. Music.*

> This is now bone of thy bones,
> And flesh of thy flesh;
> She shall be called . . . Woman,
> Because she was taken out of Man.

Wake up, Adam. *Adam opens his eyes and sits up. Eve moves out of the darkness, and they look at each other. Her skin too is covered with shadow-marks. God walks around her, inspecting her.* Hmmmm. Very nice. *To Adam*: What do you say? *Music dies off.*

ADAM, *nervously:* Well . . . she certainly is *different*.

GOD: Is that all?

ADAM: Oh, Lord, she's perfect! *But he is still uneasy.*

GOD: I think so too.

ADAM: Me too.

GOD: Huh! I don't know how I do it! What would you like to call her?

ADAM: Eve.

GOD: Eve! Lovely name. *Takes her hand.* Now dear, you will notice many different kinds of animals in this garden. Each has its inborn rule. The bee will not eat meat; the elephant will not sing and fish have no interest in flowers. —Those are apples on that tree; you will not eat them.

EVE: Why?

ADAM: That's the rule!

GOD: Be patient, Adam, she's very new. *To Eve.* Perhaps the day will come when I can give you a fuller explanation; for the moment, we'll put it this way. That is the Tree of Knowledge, Knowledge of Good and Evil. All that you have here springs from my love for you; out of love for me you will not eat of that tree or you will surely die. Not right away, but sometime. Now tell me, Eve—when you look at that tree, what do you think of?

EVE, *looks up at the tree:* . . . God?

ADAM: She got it!

GOD: That's exactly the point, dear. *Takes both their hands.* Now be glad of one another. And remember—if you eat of that tree you shall surely die. Not right away, but sometime. If you stay clear of it, everything will go on just as it is, forever. Eve?

EVE: Yes, Lord.

GOD: Adam?

ADAM: Yes, Lord.

GOD: It is all yours, my children, till the end of time.

He walks away and vanishes. Adam and Eve turn from God and face each other. They smile tentatively. Examine each other's hands, breasts. He sniffs her. Sniffs closer.

ADAM: You smell differently than I do.

EVE: You do too.

He kisses her lips. Then she kisses his. They smile. He gives a little wave.

ADAM: Well . . . maybe I'll see you again sometime. I feel like lying down over there.

EVE: I do too!

ADAM, *halting*: You do?

She stretches out.

EVE: I think I have the same thoughts you do.

ADAM, *deciding to test this*: Are you a little thirsty?

EVE: Mmhm.

ADAM: Me too. And a little hungry?

EVE: Mmhm.

ADAM: Well, that's nice. Here, want a fig?

EVE: I just felt like a fig! *They chew.*

ADAM: We can go swimming later, if you like.

EVE: Fine! That's just what I was thinking. *They lie in silence.*

ADAM: Beautiful, isn't it?

EVE: Oh, ya. Is it all right to ask—

ADAM: What?

EVE:—what you do all day?

ADAM: Well, up till recently I've been naming things. But that's practically over now. See that up there? *She looks up.* I named that a pomegranate.

EVE: Pomewhat?

ADAM: Pomegranate.

EVE: That doesn't look like a pomegranate.

ADAM: Of course its a pomegranate. *He fetches her one.* Here, eat one, you'll see. As you're spitting out the seeds it feels like "pomegranate, pomegranate, pomegranate." *She bites into it. As she spits out seeds.* Granate, granate, granate. . . .

EVE, *chewing, spitting out seeds*: Say . . . you're right, you're right.

ADAM: That's better.

EVE—*she suddenly plucks something out of his hair and holds it between her fingers*: What's this?

ADAM: That? That's a prndn. *He scratches himself.* It's one of the first things I named.

EVE: This you named a prndn?

ADAM, *with a tingle of alarm*: Now look, woman, once a thing is named, it's *named*.

EVE, *hurt, surprised*: Oh.

ADAM—*conviction failing, he turns back to her*: Why? What should I call it?

EVE: Well, to *me*, this is a louse.

ADAM: Saaay! No wonder I woke up full of L's this morning! *With a happy laugh, she eats the louse.* Isn't it marvelous how we both have exactly the same thoughts, pretty near!

EVE, *chewing*: Yes. *He stares ahead, considering for a moment, then, to show off, he spreads his arms and stands on one foot.* So what do you do all day?

ADAM: Sometimes I do this. Or this. *He rolls onto his head and does a headstand. She watches for a moment. His headstand collapses.* Why? Do you have something in mind?

EVE: I think I do, but I don't know what it is. Say, that bush!

ADAM: What about it?

EVE: I just saw it growing!

ADAM: Oh, sure. Listen . . . do you hear?

EVE: Yes. What is that sound?

ADAM: That's the sound of sunset.

EVE: And that crackling?

ADAM: A shadow is moving across dry leaves.

EVE: What is that piping sound?

ADAM: Two trout are talking in the river.

EVE, *looking upward*: Something has exhaled.

ADAM: God is sighing.

EVE: Something is rising and falling.

ADAM: That's the footsteps of an angel walking through the vines. Come, I'll show you the pool.

EVE, *getting up*: I was just thinking that!

ADAM: Good for you! I'll teach you to ride my alligators! *With a comradely arm over her shoulder he walks her out, as angels Chemuel, Azrael, and Raphael enter on the platform.*

CHEMUEL: Did you ever see anything so sweet?

RAPHAEL: Look at him putting a plum in her mouth! How lovely!

God enters on the platform.

CHEMUEL: She's adorable! Lord, you've done it again. *God, however, has left the group and stands in deep thought, apart.* Everybody! Halllllll-elujah!

ANGELS, *singing Handel*: Hallelujah, hallelujah . . .

A full-blown orchestra and mighty chorus erupt from the air in accompaniment.

GOD, *motioning them out*: Excuse me! A little later, perhaps. I'd like a few words with Lucifer.

CHEMUEL, *kissing God's hand, as they leave*: Congratulations, Lord!

RAPHAEL: We'll bring the full chorus tonight!

Alone, God looks down at the earth, as Lucifer enters.

GOD: All right, go ahead, say it.

LUCIFER: Nothing for me to say, Lord. *He points below.* You see it as well as I.

GOD, *looking down, shaking His head*: What did I do wrong?

LUCIFER: Why look at it that way? They're beautiful, they help each other, they praise You every few minutes—

GOD: Lucifer, they don't multiply.

LUCIFER: Maybe give them a few more years. . . .

GOD: But there's no sign of anything. Look at them—the middle of a perfect, moonlit night, and they're playing handball.

LUCIFER: Well, You wanted them innocent.

GOD: Every once in a while, though, he does seem to get aroused.

LUCIFER: Aroused, yes, but what's the good if he doesn't get it in the right place? And when he does, she walks off to pick a flower or something.

GOD: I can't figure that out. *Pause. They stare down.*

LUCIFER: Of course, You could always—*He breaks off.*

GOD: What?

LUCIFER: Look, I don't want to mix in, and then You'll say I'm criticizing everything—

GOD: I don't know why I stand for your superciliousness.

LUCIFER: At least I don't bore You like the rest of these spirits.

GOD: Sometimes I'd just as soon you did. What have you got in mind?

LUCIFER: Now, remember, You asked me.

GOD: What have you got in mind!

LUCIFER: You see? You're mad already.

GOD, *roaring furiously*: I am not mad!

LUCIFER: All right, all right. You could take her back and restring her insides. Reroute everything, so wherever he goes in it connects to the egg.

GOD: No-no-no, I don't want to fool with that. She's perfect now; I'm not tearing her apart again. Out of the question.

LUCIFER: Well, then, You've only got one other choice. You've got to thin out the innocence down there. *God turns to him suspiciously.* See? You're giving me that look again; whatever I say, You turn it into some kind of a plot. Like when You made that fish with the fur on. Throw him in the ocean, and all the angels run around screaming hosannas. *I* come and tell You the thing's drowned, and You're insulted.

GOD: Yes. But I—I've stopped making fish with fur any more.

LUCIFER: But before I can penetrate with a fact I've got to go through hell.

GOD—*He suddenly points down*: He's putting his arm around her. *Lucifer looks down.* Lucifer! *They both stretch over the edge to see better.* Lucifer!! *Suddenly His expression changes to incredulity, then anger, and He throws up His hands in futile protest.* Where in the world does he get those stupid ideas!

LUCIFER, *still looking down*: Now he's going to sleep.

GOD: Oh, dear, dear, dear, dear. *He sits disconsolately.*

LUCIFER: Lord, the problem down there is that You've made it all so perfect. Everything they look at is not only good, it's equally good. The sun is good, rats are good, fleas are good, the moon, lions, athlete's foot—every single thing is just as good as every other thing. Because, naturally, You created everything, so everything's as attractive as everything else.

GOD: What's so terrible about perfection? Except that you can't stand it?

LUCIFER: Well, simply—if You want him to go into her, into the right place, and stay there long enough, You'll have to make that part better.

GOD: I am not remaking that woman.

LUCIFER: It's not necessary. All I'm saying is that sex has to be made not just good, but—well, terrific. Right now he'd just as soon pick his nose. In other words, You've got to rivet his attention on that one place.

GOD: How would I do that?

LUCIFER: Well, let's look at it. What is the one thing that

makes him stop whatever he's doing and pay strict attention?

GOD: What?

LUCIFER: You, Lord. Soon as You appear, he, so to speak, comes erect. Give sex that same sort of holiness in his mind, the same sort of hope that is never discouraged and never really fulfilled, the same fear of being unacceptable. Make him feel toward sex as he feels toward You, and You're in —*unbeschreiblich!* Between such high promise and deadly terror, he won't be able to think of anything else.

Pause.

GOD: How?

LUCIFER: Well . . . *He hesitates a long moment, until God slowly turns to him with a suspicious look.* All right, look— there's no way around it, I simply have to talk about those apples.

GOD, *stamps His foot and stands, strides up and down, trying to control His temper*: Lucifer!

LUCIFER: I refuse to believe that man's only way to demonstrate his love for God is to refuse to eat some fruit! That kind of game is simply unworthy of my father!

GOD, *angered*: Really now!

LUCIFER: Forgive me, sir, but I am useless to you if I don't speak my mind. May I tell you why *I* think You planted that tree in the garden? *God is silent, but consenting, even if unwillingly.* Objectively speaking, it *is* senseless. You wanted Adam's praise for everything You made, absolutely innocent of any doubt about Your goodness. Why, then, plant a fruit which can only make him wise, sophisticated, and analytical? May I continue? *God half-willingly nods.* He certainly will begin to question everything if he eats an apple, but why is that necessarily bad? *God looks surprised, angering.* He'll not only marvel that the flower blooms, he will ask why and discover chlorophyll—and bless You for chlorophyll. He'll not only praise You that food makes him strong, he will discover his bile duct and praise You for his pancreas. He may lose his innocence, but the more he learns of Your secrets, the more reasons he will have to praise You. And that is why, quite without consciously knowing it, You planted that tree there. It was Your fantastic inner urge to magnify Your glory to the last degree. In six words, Lord, You wanted full credit for everything.

GOD: He must never eat those apples.

LUCIFER: Then why have You tempted him? What is the point?

GOD: I wanted him to wake each morning, look at that tree, and say, "For God's sake I won't eat these apples." Not even one.

LUCIFER: Fine. But with that same absence of curiosity he is not investigating Eve.

GOD: But the other animals manage.

LUCIFER: Their females go into heat, and the balloon goes up. But Eve is ready almost any time, and that means no time. It's part of that whole dreadful uniformity down there.

GOD: They are my children; I don't want them to know evil.

LUCIFER: Why call it evil? One apple, and he'll know the difference between good and better. And once he knows that, he'll be all over her. *He looks down.* Look, he's kissing a tree. You see? The damned fool has no means of discriminating.

GOD, *looking down*: Well, he should kiss trees too.

LUCIFER: Fine. If that's the way You feel, You've got Adam and Eve, and it'll be a thousand years before you're a grandfather. *He stands.* Think it over. I'd be glad to go down and—*God gives him a look.* I'm only trying to help!

GOD: Lucifer, I'm way ahead of you.

LUCIFER: Lord, that's inevitable.

GOD: Stay away from that tree.

LUCIFER, *with a certain evasiveness*: Whatever You say, sir. May I go now?

GOD, *after a pause*: Don't have the illusion that I am in conflict about this; I mean, don't decide to go down there and do Me a favor, or something. I know perfectly well why I put that tree there.

LUCIFER, *surprised*: Really!

GOD: Yes, really. I am in perfect control over my unconscious, friend. It was not to tempt Adam; it's I who was tempted. I finished him and I saw he was beautiful, and for a moment I loved him beyond anything I had ever made— and I thought, maybe I should let him see through the rose petal to its chemistry, the formation of amino acids to the secrets of life. His simple praise for surfaces made me impatient to show him the physics of My art, which would raise him to a god.

LUCIFER: Why'd You change Your mind?

GOD: Because I thought of what became of you. The one angel who really understands biology and physics, the one I loved before all the rest and took such care to teach—and you can't take a breath without thinking how to overthrow Me and take over the universe!

LUCIFER: Lord, I only wanted them to know more, the more to praise You!

GOD: The more they know, the less they will need Me, Lucifer; you know that as well as I! And that's all you're after, to grind away their respect for Me. "Give them an apple!" If it weren't for the Law of the Conservation of Energy I would destroy you! Don't go near that tree or those dear people—not in any form, you hear? They are innocent, and innocent they will remain till I turn out the lights forever!

God goes out. Lucifer is alone.

LUCIFER: Now what is He *really* saying? He put it there to tempt *Himself!* Therefore He's not of one mind about innocence; and how could He be when innocence blinds Adam to half the wonders He has made? I will help the Lord. Yes, that's the only way to put it; I'm His helper. I open up the marvels He dares not show, and thereby magnify His glory. In short, I disobey what He says and carry out what He means, and if that's evil, it's only to do good. Strange—I never felt so close to my creator as I do right now! Once Adam eats, he'll multiply, and Lucifer completes the lovely world of God! Oh, praise the Lord who gave me all this insight! My fight with Him is over! Now evil be my good, and Eve and Adam multiply in blessed sin! Make way, dumb stars, the world of man begins!

He exits as light rises on Paradise, where Eve is bent over from the waist, examining a—to us invisible—turtle. Adam enters. His attention is caught by her raised buttocks, and he approaches, halts, and stares—then looks off, puzzled by an idea he can't quite form in his mind. Giving it up, he asks . . .

ADAM: You want to play volleyball?

Lucifer enters.

LUCIFER: Good evening.

ADAM: Good evening. *He nervously nudges Eve, who now stands up. Something in Lucifer moves something in her.*

EVE: Oh!

Lucifer exchanges a deep glance with her, then moves, glancing about and then turns back to Adam.

LUCIFER: Had enough?

EVE: Enough of what?

LUCIFER: You don't imagine, do you, that God intended you to lie around like this forever?

ADAM: We're going swimming later.

LUCIFER: Swimming! What about making something of yourselves?

ADAM: Making some . . . ?

LUCIFER, *with a quick glance about for God*: I'm a little

short of time, Adam. By the way, my name is Lucifer. The archangel?

ADAM, *impressed*: Ohhh! I'm very pleased to meet you. This is my wife, Eve.

EVE: How do you do?

LUCIFER, *taking her hand with a little pressure*: Awfully nice to meet you, Eve. Tell me, you ever hold your breath?

ADAM: Oh, sure, she does that a lot. Show him, Eve. *She inhales and holds it.* She can do that till she turns blue. *Eve lets out the air.*

EVE: I can really turn blue if I want to.

LUCIFER: And why does that happen?

ADAM: Because God makes it.

LUCIFER: But how, dear?

ADAM: How should she know?

LUCIFER: But God *wants* her to know.

ADAM: But why didn't He tell us?

LUCIFER: He's trying to tell you; that's why I've come; I am the Explainer. Adam, the fact is that God gives His most important commands through His silences. For example, there is nothing He feels more passionate about than that you begin to multiply.

EVE: Really?

LUCIFER: Of course. That's why that tree is there.

EVE: We multiply with the tree?

LUCIFER: No, but if you eat the fruit you'll know how. He just can't bring Himself to say it, you see.

EVE: Is that so!

ADAM: Now, wait a minute, excuse me. We're not even supposed to *think* about that tree.

EVE: Say, that's right. In fact, lately, that's practically all I do is go around not thinking about it.

LUCIFER: Oh, you find that's getting difficult?

EVE: No, but it takes up so much time.

ADAM: It's because we'll die if we eat those things. *Lucifer reaches up, takes the apple.* You better watch out, they're not good for you—Don't! *Lucifer bites into the apple, chews. They watch him, wide-eyed.* Oh, I know why, it's that you're an angel!

LUCIFER: You could be too.

ADAM, *worried*: Angels?

LUCIFER: Absolutely. Now listen carefully, because this is fairly deep and I may have to leave any minute. You know by now why the Lord put you in this lovely garden.

ADAM: To praise everything.

LUCIFER: Right. Now what if I told you that there are a number of things you've been leaving out?

ADAM, *shocked*: Oh, no! I praise absolutely everything.

LUCIFER, *pointing to his penis*: And what about this thing here? Do you praise Him for that?

ADAM, *looking down at himself*: Well, not in particular, but I include it in.

LUCIFER: But how can you when you don't know what it's for?

EVE: He pees that way.

LUCIFER: Pees! That is so incidental it's not even worth mentioning. *To Adam*: You have no idea, do you?

ADAM: Well . . . ahh . . .

LUCIFER: Yes?

ADAM: I'm only guessing, but sometimes it makes me feel—

LUCIFER: Feel what?

ADAM: Well . . . kind of sporty?

LUCIFER: Adam! God has made you in His image, given you His body. How dare you refuse to understand the very best part of it? Now you will eat this apple.

ADAM: Angel, please—I really don't feel I should.

LUCIFER, *holding the apple to Adam's tightly shut lips*: You must! Could I make this offer without God's permission?

EVE: Say, that's right!

LUCIFER: Of course it's right! I mean nothing happens He doesn't want to happen—*n'est-ce pas?* Now, you take one bite, and I promise you will understand everything. Adam, open your mouth and you will become—*he glances quickly about, lowers his voice*—like God.

ADAM: Like *God*! You should never say a thing like that!

LUCIFER: You're not even living like animals!

ADAM: I don't want to hear any more! He said it in plain Hebrew, don't eat those apples, and that's it! I'm going swimming. Eve?

EVE, *extending her hand to Lucifer*: Very nice to have met you.

LUCIFER, *slowly running his eyes from her feet to her face*: Likewise.

A strange sensation emanates from his eyes, and she slowly looks down at her body.

ADAM: Eve?

She unwillingly breaks from Lucifer, and they leave. Lucifer looks at the apple in his hand and takes a big bite. He stands there chewing thoughtfully. Offstage a splash is heard. A pause. Eve returns, glancing behind her, and hurries to Lucifer.

EVE: There's only one thing I wonder if you could tell me.

LUCIFER: I love questions, my dear. What is it?

EVE—*she looks down at herself, pointing*: Why has he got that thing and I don't?

LUCIFER: Isn't it funny? I knew you were going to ask that question.

EVE: Well, I mean, is it going to grow on later?

LUCIFER: Never.

EVE: Why?

LUCIFER, *offering her his apple*: Take a bite, Eve, and everything will clear up.

EVE—*she accepts the apple, looks at it*: It smells all right.

LUCIFER: Of course. It *is* all right.

EVE: Maybe just a little bite.

LUCIFER: Better make it medium. You have an awful lot to learn, dear.

EVE: Well . . . here goes! *She bites and chews, her eyes widening, her body moving sinuously. A dread sound fills the air. She approaches him.*

LUCIFER, *retreating*: 'Fraid I've got to leave, dear.

EVE: You going *now*?

LUCIFER: Oh, yes, right now! But I'll be around.

He hurries off, glancing behind with trepidation. She stands there staring. She feels her body, her breasts, her face, awakening to herself. She starts her hand down to her genitals and inhales a surprised breath. Adam enters. The sound goes silent.

ADAM: Where were you? Come on, the water's perfect! . . . Eve? *She turns to him.* What's the matter? *She sensuously touches his arm and puts it around her.* What are you doing? *She smashes her lips against his.* What is this? *She holds her apple before his face.*

EVE: Eat it.

ADAM: Eve!

EVE: It's marvelous! Please, a bite, a bite!

ADAM: But God said—

EVE: I'm God.

ADAM: You're what?

EVE: He is in me! He'll be in you! I never felt like this! I am the best thing that ever happened! Look at me! Adam, don't you see me?

ADAM: Well, sure, I—

EVE: You're not looking at me!

ADAM: Of course I'm looking at you!

EVE: But you're not *seeing* me! You don't see anything!

ADAM: Why? I see the trees, the sky—

EVE: You wouldn't see anything else if you were seeing me.

ADAM: How's that possible?

EVE: Say "Ahh."

ADAM: Ahh.

She suddenly pushes the apple into his mouth.

EVE: Chew! Swallow!

He chews. The dread sound again. She watches. He looks down at his penis. Then to her. Then up at her face, astonished. He starts to reach for her.

VOICE OF GOD, *echoing through the theater on the PA system:* WHERE ART THOU! *They both retract, glancing desperately around. They rush about, trying to hide from each other.* WHERE ART THOU!

ADAM: Here, quick! Put something on! *He hands her a leaf, which she holds in front of her.* Gee, you know you look even better with that leaf on—

EVE, *looking off*: He's coming!

They disappear. God enters.

GOD: Where art thou?

ADAM, *still unseen*: Here, Lord. *God turns, looking around. Adam emerges. He is wearing a large leaf. Nervously apologizing.* I heard Thy voice in the garden and I was afraid, because I was naked; and I hid myself. *Eve emerges.*

GOD: Who told thee that thou wast naked?

ADAM: Who told me?

GOD: Who told thee! You didn't know you were naked!

ADAM, *appalled, looking down at himself*: Say, that's right.

GOD, *mimicking him*: "Say, that's right." You ate the apple!

ADAM: She made me.

EVE: I couldn't help it. A snake came. *To Adam*: Wasn't he a snake?

ADAM: Like a snake, ya.

GOD: That son of a . . . *Calling out*: Lucifer, I get my hands on you . . . !

EVE: But why put the tree here if You . . . ?

GOD: *You're* questioning *Me*! Who the hell do you think you are? I put the tree here so there would be at least one thing you shouldn't think about! So, unlike the animals, you should exercise a little self-control.

EVE: Oh!

GOD: "Oh," she says. I'll give you an "Oh" that you'll wish you'd never been born! But first I'm going to fix it between you and snakes. Serpent, because thou hast done this,

> Thou art cursed above all cattle,
> And above every beast of the field;
> And I will put enmity between thee and woman—
> That means all women will hate snakes.
> Or almost all.

You see? It's already impossible to make an absolute statement around here! You bad girl, look what you did to Me!

EVE, *covering her face*: I'm ashamed.

GOD: Ashamed! You don't know the half of it.

> I will greatly multiply thy sorrow and thy conception;
> In sorrow thou shalt bring forth children—

EVE: Oh God!

> GOD: And thy desire shall be to thy husband
> And he shall rule over thee.

No more equals, you hear? He's the boss forever. Pull up your leaf. *He turns to Adam.* And as for you, schmuck!

> Cursed is the ground for thy sake,
> In sorrow shalt thou eat of it all the days of thy life.
> Thorns and thistles shall it bring forth to thee;
> No more going around just picking up lunch.
> In the sweat of thy face shalt thou eat bread,
> Till thou return unto the ground;
> Yes, my friend, now there is time and age and death,

No more living forever. You got it?
For dust thou art.
And unto dust shalt thou return.

ADAM—*he sobs*: What am I doing? What's this water?

GOD: You're weeping, my son, those are your first tears;
There will be more before you're finished.
Now you have become as one of us,
A little lower than the angels,
Because now you know good and evil.
Adam and Eve? Get out of the Garden.

ADAM: Out where?

GOD, *pointing*: There!

ADAM: But that's a desert!

GOD: Right! It wasn't good enough for you here? Go and see how you make out on your own.

ADAM: God. Dear God, isn't there any way we can get back in? I don't want to be ashamed, I don't want to be so full of sadness. It was so wonderful here, we were both so innocent!

GOD: Out! You know too much to live in Eden.

ADAM: But I am ignorant!

GOD: Knowing you are ignorant is too much to know.
The lion and the elephant, the spider and the mouse—
They will remain, but they know My perfection
Without knowing it. You ate what I forbade,
You yearned for what you were not
And thus laid a judgment on My work.
I Am What I Am What I Am, but it was not enough;

The warmth in the sand, the coolness of water,
The coming and going of day and night—
It was not enough to live in these things.
You had to have power, and power is in you now,
But not Eden any more. Listen, Adam. Listen, Eve.
Can you hear the coming of night?

ADAM—*surprised, he raises his hand*: Why . . . no!

GOD: Can you hear the sound of shadows on the leaves?

EVE, *with immense loss and wonder*: No!

God turns his back on them, hurt, erect.

EVE: Where is the voice of the trout talking in the river?

ADAM: Where are the footsteps of angels walking through the vines?

On the verge of weeping, they are turning to catch the sounds they knew, deaf to the world. Light is playing on them as instruments are heard playing a lugubrious tune. They dejectedly leave Paradise.

A sad bassoon solo emerges, played by Raphael. God, hands behind his back, turns to Raphael, Chemuel, and Azrael, who enter together.

GOD: That is the most depressing instrument I have ever heard.

RAPHAEL, *the bassoonist, protesting*: But You invented it, Lord.

GOD: I can't imagine how I could have thought of such a thing.

CHEMUEL: It was just after Eve ate the apple. You were

very down. And You said, "I think I will invent the bassoon."

GOD: Well, put it away, Raphael.

AZRAEL: Look at Adam and Eve down there. All they do any more is screw.

CHEMUEL: Maybe we ought to talk about something cheerful.

GOD: Do that, yes.

Pause. The angels think.

CHEMUEL: I think the Rocky Mountains are the best yet! *God turns to him, pained.* I mean the way they go up.

RAPHAEL: And then the way they go down.

GOD: I'm afraid that Lucifer was the only one of you who knew how to carry on a conversation.

AZRAEL, *a fierce fellow, deep-throated*: I would like to kill Adam and Eve.

GOD: That's natural, Azrael, as the Angel of Death, but I'm not ready for that yet.

AZRAEL: They like to swim; I could drown them. Or push them over a cliff—

GOD, *pained*: Don't say those things, stop it.

AZRAEL: I have to say, Lord, I warned You at the time: You mustn't make a creature that looks like You, or You'll *never* let me kill him.

CHEMUEL: It was such a pleasure with the lions and the gorillas.

GOD: Yes, but—*he looks down at the earth*—when they're good it makes me feel so marvelous.

AZRAEL: But how often are they good?

GOD: I know, but when they praise My name and all that. There's nothing like it. When they send up those hallelujahs from Notre Dame—

AZRAEL: Notre Dame!

RAPHAEL: Lord, Notre Dame isn't for six thousand years.

GOD: I know, but I'm looking forward. *He stands, shocked, His eye caught by something below.* Look at that! How do they think up such positions?

AZRAEL: I don't understand why You let them go on offending You like this. You called back other mistakes—the fish with fur who drowned—

CHEMUEL: And the beetle who hiccupped whenever it snowed.

AZRAEL: Why don't You let me go down and wipe them out?

GOD: They are the only ones who need Me.

CHEMUEL: Sure! Give them a chance.

GOD: I'll never forget the first time I realized what I meant to them. It was the first time Adam laid her down and went into her. She closed her eyes, and she began to breathe so deeply I thought she'd faint, or die, or explode. And suddenly she cried out, "Oh dear God!" I have never heard My name so genuinely praised.

AZRAEL: I find the whole spectacle disgusting.

GOD: I know. It's the worst thing that ever happened. *He is in conflict, staring.* It can't go on this way; I must have it out with Lucifer.

ALL: Lucifer!

GOD, *energetically*: I have never before been in conflict with Myself. Look at it; My poor, empty Eden; the ripened peach falls uneaten to the ground, and My two idiotic darlings roam the desert scrounging for a crust. It has definitely gone wrong. And not one of you has an idea worth talking about. Clear away; I must decide.

CHEMUEL: Decide what, Lord?

GOD: I don't know yet, but a decision is definitely rising in Me. And that was the one thing Lucifer always knew—the issue. Go. *Chemuel throws up his hands.*

ALL, *singing*: Hallelujah, hallelujah . . .

The angels are walking out.

GOD. One more.

ALL: Hallelujah!

They go. God is alone. He concentrates. Lucifer appears.

LUCIFER, *wary, looking for cues to God's attitude*: Thank You, Father. I have been waiting. I am ready to face my ordeal.

GOD: Lucifer, I have been struggling to keep from destroying you. The Law of the Conservation of Energy does not protect an angel from being broken into small pieces and sprinkled over the Atlantic Ocean.

LUCIFER: Wouldn't that just spread him around, though?

GOD: What restrains me is a feeling that somewhere in the universe a stupendous event has occurred. For an instant it made Me terribly happy. I thought it might be the icecaps, but they're not really working out.

LUCIFER: Trouble?

GOD: There is a definite leak.

LUCIFER: Can You repair it?

GOD: I've decided to let them run. It will mean a collection of large lakes across North America, and some in Europe.

LUCIFER: Oh, Father, surely You planned it that way.

GOD: I see now that I probably did; but frankly I wasn't thinking of the lakes; I simply felt there should be icecaps on both poles. But that's the way it is—one thing always leads to another.

LUCIFER: Then you must already know the fantastic news I've brought You.

GOD, *staring for his thought*: I undoubtedly do. *At a loss*: Happy news.

LUCIFER: Glorious.

GOD: I knew it! In the very midst of all my disappointments I suddenly felt a sort of . . . hopeful silence.

LUCIFER: The silent seed of Adam squirming into Eve's ovarian tube.

GOD: *striking His forehead*: Aaaaah! Of course! And the ovum?

LUCIFER: Has been fertilized.

GOD: And has attached itself . . .

LUCIFER: To the womb. It is holding on nicely.

GOD: Then so far—

LUCIFER: So good. I can't see any reason to worry.

GOD: *clapping His hands*: My first upright pregnancy! *Worried*: Maybe she ought to lie down more.

LUCIFER: Lord, she could stand on her head and not lose it.

GOD: And how is she feeling?

LUCIFER: I thought I'd ask You about that. She is slightly nauseated in the mornings.

GOD: That is partly disgust with herself. At least I hope so. But it is also the blood supply diverting to the womb.

LUCIFER: I never thought of that! In any case, it works.

GOD: How utterly, utterly superb.

LUCIFER: Oh, dear Father, ever since my interview with Eve I've been terrified You'd never speak to me again. And now when I so want to thank You properly, all metaphor, simile, and image scatter before this victory of ours. *God becomes alert*. Like the firm cheek of heaven, the wall of her womb nuzzles the bud of the first son of man.

GOD: Say that again?

LUCIFER: Like the firm—

GOD: No, before that.

Slight pause.

LUCIFER: But surely it was all according to plan?

GOD, *peering at him*: According to . . . ?

LUCIFER: It was supposed to happen through me. Of course, I am perfectly aware that I merely acted as Your agent.

GOD: Not on your life! They would have made it in Paradise, clean and innocent, and with My blessing instead of My curse!

LUCIFER: But the fact is, they were not making it!

GOD: They might have by accident!

LUCIFER: Father, I can't believe a technicality is more important than this service to Your cause!

GOD: Technicality! I am going to condemn you, Lucifer.

LUCIFER: Dear God, for what? For making You a grandfather?

GOD: I forbade that apple! Nobody violates a Commandment, I don't care how good it comes out!

LUCIFER: You mean the letter of the law is more important than the survival of the human race? *God is silent. A smile breaks onto Lucifer's face.* This is a test, isn't it? You're testing me? *God is inscrutable.* That's all right, don't answer. Now I will confess myself and prove that I finally understand my part in the Plan.

GOD: What Plan? What are you talking about?

LUCIFER: Your hidden Plan for operating the world. All my life, sir, I've had the feeling that I was somehow . . . a *useless angel.* I look at Azrael, so serious and grave, perfect for the Angel of Death. And our sweet Chemuel—

exactly right for the Angel of Mercy. But when I tried to examine *my* character, I could never find any. Gorgeous profile, superb intelligence, but what was Lucifer *for*? Am I boring You?

GOD: Not at all.

LUCIFER, *worried*: How do you mean that? *God simply looks at him.* Good, good—don't make it easy for me. I will now explain about the apple. You see, I'd gone down there to help you, but she took one bite and that innocent stare erupted with such carnal appetite that I began to wonder, was it possible I had actually done something— *He breaks off.*

GOD: Evil?

LUCIFER: Oh, that terrible word! But now I will face it! *The desperate yet joyful confession.* Father, I've *always* had certain impulses that mystified me. If I saw my brother angels soaring upwards, my immediate impulse was to go down. A raspberry cane bends to the right, I'd find myself leaning left. Others praise the forehead, I am drawn to the ass. Holes—I don't want to leave anything out—I adore holes. Every hole is precious to me. I'll go even further— in excrement, decay, the intestine of the world is my stinking desire. You ever hear anything so straightforwardly disgusting? I tell you I have felt so worthless, I was often ready to cut my throat. But Eve is pregnant now, and I see the incredible, hidden truth.

GOD: Which is?

LUCIFER: How can I be rotten? How else but through my disobedience was Eve made pregnant with mankind? How dare I hate myself? Not only am I not rotten—I am God's corrective symmetry, that festering embrace which keeps His world from impotent virtue. And once I saw that, I saw Your purpose working through me and I nearly wept with self-respect. And I fell in love—with both of us. *Slight pause. God is motionless.* Well, that's—the general idea, right?

GOD: Lucifer, you are a degenerate! You are a cosmic pervert!

LUCIFER: But God in Heaven, who made me this way?

God whacks him across the face; Lucifer falls to his knees.

GOD: Don't you ever, ever say that.

LUCIFER: Adonoi elohaenu, adonoi echaud. Father, I know Your anger is necessary, but my love stands fast!

GOD: Love! The only love you know is for yourself! You think I haven't seen you standing before a mirror whole years at a time!

LUCIFER: I have, Lord, admiring Your handiwork.

GOD: How can you lie like this and not even blush!

LUCIFER: All right! *He stands up. Now* I will tell You the truth! *At the pinnacle*: Lord, I am ready to take my place beside the throne.

GOD: Beside the *what*?

LUCIFER: Why, the throne, Lord. At Your right hand. If not the right, then the left. I can suggest a title: Minister of Excremental Matters. I can walk with a limp, now watch this. *He walks, throwing one leg out spastically.*

GOD: What is this?

LUCIFER: And I do a tic, You see? *He does a wild tic as he walks crazily.*

GOD: What are you doing?

LUCIFER: I'll stutter, too. *Horribly:* Whoo, wha—mun-nnn—

GOD: What is this?

LUCIFER: I'll wear a hunch back and masturbate incessantly, eternal witness that God loves absolutely everything He made! What a *lesson*! But before You answer—the point, the far-reaching ultimate, is that this will change the future. Do You remember the future, Lord?

GOD: Of course I remember the future.

LUCIFER: It is a disaster; it is one ghastly war after another down through the centuries.

GOD: You can never change the future. The past, yes, but not the future.

LUCIFER: How do you change the past?

GOD: Why, the past is always changing—nobody remembers anything. But the future can no more be turned away than the light flowing off the moon.

LUCIFER: Unless we stood together, Lord, You immaculate on Your throne, absolutely good, and I beside You, perfectly evil. Father and son, the two inseparable buddies. *God is caught by it.* There could never, never be war! You see it, I can see You see it! If good and evil stand as one, what'll they have to fight about? What army could ever mobilize if on all the flags was written: "For God and Country and the Stinking Devil"? Without absolute righteousness there can never be a war! We will flummox the generals! Father, you are a handshake away from a second Paradise! Peace on earth to the end of time. *God is peering, feverish.* And that, sir, is your entire plan for me as I see it.

GOD: In other words, I would no longer be absolutely right.

LUCIFER: Just in public, sir. Privately, of course—*a gesture connecting them*—we know what's what.

GOD: We do.

LUCIFER: Oh, Lord, I have no thought of . . . actually—

GOD: Sharing power.

LUCIFER: God forbid. I'm speaking purely of the image.

GOD: But in reality . . .

LUCIFER: Nothing's changed. You're good, and I'm bad. It's just that to the public—

GOD: We will appear to be—

LUCIFER: Yes.

GOD: Equal.

LUCIFER: Not morally equal. Just equally real. Because if I'm sitting beside You in Heaven—

GOD: Then I must love you.

LUCIFER: Exactly. And if God can love the Devil, He can love absolutely anybody.

GOD: *That's* certainly true, yes.

LUCIFER: So people would never come to hate themselves, and there's the end of guilt. Another Eden, and everybody innocent again.

Pause.

GOD: Operationally speaking—

LUCIFER: Yes.

GOD: Yes *sir.*

LUCIFER: Yes sir. Excuse me.

GOD: In cases of lying, cheating, fornication, murder, and so on—you mean they are no longer to be judged?

LUCIFER: Oh, on the contrary! Between the two of us *no one* will escape the judgment of Heaven. I'll judge the bad people, and you judge the good.

GOD: But who would try to be good if it's just as good to be bad?

LUCIFER: And will the bad be good for fear of your judgment? So you may as well let them be bad and the good be good, and either way they'll all love God because they'll know that God . . . loves . . . me. Sir, I am ready to take my place. Between the two of us we'll have mankind mouse-trapped.

GOD: Yes. *Slight pause.* There is only one problem.

LUCIFER: But basically that's the Plan, isn't it?

GOD: There is a problem.

LUCIFER: What's that?

GOD, *looking straight at him*: I don't love you.

LUCIFER, *shocked—he can hardly speak*: You can't mean that.

GOD: Afraid I do.

LUCIFER: Well. *He gives a deflated laugh.* This is certainly a surprise.

GOD: I see that. And it is fundamentally why we can never sit together. Nothing is real to you. Except your appetite for distinction and power. I've been waiting for some slightest sign of repentance for what you did to Paradise, but there's nothing, is there? Instead, I'm to join you in a cosmic comedy where good and evil are the same. It doesn't occur to you that I am unable to share the bench with the very incarnation of all I despise?

LUCIFER: I can't believe You'd let Your feelings stand in the way of peace.

GOD: But that is why I am perfect—I *am* my feelings.

LUCIFER: You don't think that's a limitation?

GOD: It certainly is. I am perfectly limited. Where evil begins, I end. When good loves evil, it is no longer good, and if God could love the Devil, then God has died. And that is precisely what you're after, isn't it?!

LUCIFER: I am after peace! Between us and mankind!

GOD: Then let there be war! Better ten thousand years of war than I should rule one instant with the help of unrighteousness!

LUCIFER: Lord God, I am holding out my hand!

GOD, *rising*: Go to Hell! Now thou art fallen in all thy
    beauty.
As the rain doth fall and green the grass
And the fish out of water suffocates,
So dost thy fall prove that there are consequences.
Now die in Heaven, Lucifer, and live in Hell
That man may ever know how good and evil separate!

LUCIFER: Lord? *He is upright, stern.* You will not take my
hand?

GOD: Never! Never, never, never!

LUCIFER: Then I will take the world. *He exits.*

GOD, *calling*: And if you ever do, I will burn it, I will flood
it out, I will leave it a dead rock spinning in silence! For
I am the Lord, and the Lord is good and only good!

    ANGELS' VOICES, *singing loudly and sharply*: Blessed
        is the Lord my God,
    Glory, glory, glory!

*God sits, cleaved by doubt. He turns His head, looking
about.*

GOD: Why do I miss him? *He stares ahead.* How strange.

CURTAIN

Act II

Darkness. The sound of a high wind. It dies off. A starry sky.

In the starlight, Adam and Eve are discovered asleep, but apart. He snores contentedly, she lies in silence on her back, her very pregnant belly arching up.

Lucifer, in black now, rises from the ground. He scans the sky for any sign of God, then looks down at the two people. In deep thought he walks to the periphery and sits, his chin on his fist, staring.

Overhead a bird begins to sing. He looks up.

LUCIFER: Oh, shut up. *The birdsong effloresces gloriously.* Will you get out of here? Go! Glorify the Lord some place else! *Flapping of wings. He follows the bird's flight overhead with his gaze.* Idiot. *Depressed, he stares ahead.* Everything I see throws up the same irrational lesson. The hungriest bird sings best. What a system! That deprivation should make music—is anarchy! And what is greatness in God's world? A peaceful snake lies dozing in the sun with no more dignity than a long worm; but let him arch his head to strike—and there, by God, is a *snake*! Yes! I have reasoned, pleaded, argued, when only murder in this world makes majesty—God's included. Was He ever Godlier, ever more my king than when He murdered my hopes?

And will I ever be more than a ridiculous angel—*he turns to Adam and Eve*—until I murder His? *He stands, goes to Eve, looks down at her.* Where is His dearest hope in all the world—but in that belly? *He suddenly raises his foot to stomp her, then retracts.* No. N-no. Let her do it. Make her do it. *He looks skyward.* Oh, the shock, the shock! If she refused the Lord the fruit of man because He made the world unreasonable! *He inspires himself, slowly sinks to the ground, and insinuates into Eve's ear:* This is a dream. *He ceremoniously lifts his hand and with his middle finger touches her forehead.* I enter the floor of thy skull. *He bends and kisses her belly.* Now, woman, help me save the world from the anarchy of God. *She inhales sensuously, and her knee rises, her cloak falling away, exposing a bare thigh.* Your time has come, dear woman. *He slides his hand along her thigh.*

EVE, *exhaling pleasurably*: Aaaaaahhh!

LUCIFER: Sssh! Don't wake up; the only safe place to have this conversation is inside your head. Am I clear in your mind? Do you remember me?

EVE: Oh, yes! When our fingers touched around the apple—

LUCIFER: Flesh to naked flesh!

EVE: And I awoke and saw myself! How beautiful I was! *She opens her eyes.*

LUCIFER: What in the world has happened to you? How'd you get so ugly?

EVE, *covering her face*: I can't stand myself!

LUCIFER: When I think how you looked in Paradise—*she weeps*—Why did you let yourself go?

EVE: Can you help me, angel? Something's got into my belly, and it keeps getting bigger.

LUCIFER: No idea what it is?

EVE: Well . . . I *have* been eating a lot of clams lately.

LUCIFER: Clams.

EVE: Sometimes it even squirms. *Lucifer looks away in thought.* Isn't that it?

LUCIFER, *turning back to her*: Like to have it out?

EVE, *clapping her hands*: Could I?

LUCIFER: But are you sure you won't change your mind afterwards?

EVE: No! I want to be as I was. Please, angel, take thy power and drive it out.

LUCIFER: Lie back, dear.

EVE: Oh, thank you, angel, I will adore you forever!

LUCIFER, *starting to spread her knees*: I certainly hope so. Now just try to relax. , . .

EVE, *on her back, facing the sky, her arms stretched upward*: Oh, won't the Lord be happy when He sees me looking good again! *Lucifer removes his hands, instantly turning away to think. She, on her back, can't see what he is doing.* Is anything happening?

LUCIFER, *drawing her upright*: Woman, I don't want you

hating me in the morning; now listen, and I will waken your mind as once I awakened your body in Paradise.

EVE: By the way, I've been wanting to ask you: did you ever come to me again—*after* Paradise?

LUCIFER, *evasively*: Why do you ask?

EVE: Near twilight, once, I was lying on my stomach, looking at my face in a pool; and suddenly a strange kind of weight pressed down on my back, and it pressed and pressed until we seemed to go tumbling out like dragonflies above the water. And in my ear a voice kept whispering, "This is God's will, darling. . . ."

LUCIFER: Which it was, at the time.

EVE, *marveling*: It was you!

LUCIFER: All me. About nine months ago.

EVE, *gleefully*: Oh, angel, that was glorious! Come, make me beautiful again! *She starts to lie back; he stops her.*

LUCIFER: You will have it out, Eve, Eve, but it's important there be no recriminations afterwards, so I'm going to tell you the truth. I have been thrown out of Heaven.

EVE: How's that possible? You're an *angel*!

LUCIFER: Dear girl, we are dealing with a spirit to whom nothing is sacred.

EVE: But why? What did you do?

LUCIFER: What He could not do. *He breaks off.*

EVE: What?

LUCIFER, *taking the plunge*: I caused you to multiply.

EVE: You mean—*she looks down at her belly*—I'm multiplying?

LUCIFER: What you have in your belly . . . is a man.

EVE: A man! *Overjoyed, she rolls back onto the ground.* In me!

LUCIFER: Remember what you said! You want it out!

EVE, *sitting up*: How is God feeling about me? Does He know?

LUCIFER: All right, then. Yes, He knows and He is ecstatic!

EVE: Oh, praise the Lord!

LUCIFER, *furiously*: Quadruple hallelujahs!

EVE: Glory to Him in the highest!

LUCIFER: Precisely. *Jabbing his finger at her*: And now I'll bet your agony begins!

EVE, *with a shock of pain*: Aaaahhhhh!

LUCIFER: Why'd you stop praising Him? *She yells in pain.* Where's the hallelujah!?

EVE: What is happening to me?

LUCIFER: What're you complaining about? You praise God, and this is what you get for it!

EVE: But why?

LUCIFER: Don't you remember Him cursing you out of Paradise?

EVE: And this—

LUCIFER: Is it, honey.

EVE, *pointing to the sleeping Adam*: But he ate the apple too!

LUCIFER: Right. And he looks better than ever.

EVE, *furiously pounding her hands on the ground*: WHY?

LUCIFER, *grabbing her face, driving his point home*: Because this is the justice of the world He made, and only you can change that world!

EVE: Angel . . . it's getting worse.

LUCIFER: Oh, it'll get worse than this, dear.

EVE: It can't get worse!

LUCIFER: Oh, yes, it can, because He's perfect, and when He makes something worse, it's *perfectly* worse!

EVE: Oh God, what have I done!

LUCIFER: You multiplied with my help, not with His, and your agony is His bureaucratic revenge. Now listen to me—

EVE: I can't stand any more! *Lashing about on the ground*: Where's a rock, I'll kill him! *With clawed hands she starts for Adam.*

LUCIFER: He is as innocent as you!

EVE, *bursting into helpless tears*: this is not *right*!

LUCIFER: Oh, woman, to hear that word at last from other lips than mine! It is not right, no—it is chaos. Eve, you are the only voice of reason God's insane world can ever have, for in you alone His chaos shows its claws. *In poene veritas*—the only truth is pain. Now mount it and take your power.

EVE: What power? I'm a grain of dust.

LUCIFER: He is pacing up and down in Heaven waiting for this child. You have in your belly the crown of God.

EVE: The crown . . . ?

LUCIFER: His highest honor is your gratitude for the agony He is giving you. He is a maniac! *He takes her hand.* You can refuse. You must deny this crown to chaos. Kill it. *He is behind her, his lips to her ear, his hand on her belly.*

> Let the serpent in again, and we'll murder him,
> And so teach the Lord His first humility.

He slips around in front of her, starting to press her back to the ground.

> Crown His vengeance on thee not with life
> But with a death; a lump of failure
> Lay before the Lord a teaching, woman—

EVE, *in conflict, resisting his pressure to lie down*; *I* teach God?

> LUCIFER: Teach God, yes!—that if men must be born
> Only in the pain of uncarned sin,
> Then there will be no men at all!
> Open to me!

He tries to spread her legs. She reaches uncertainly to his face, while trying to fend his hands off.

EVE: Angel, I'm afraid!

LUCIFER: Hold still! *He is on top of her to pin her down.*

EVE: I don't think I can do that!

LUCIFER: Open up, you bitch! *He violently tries to spread her knees; she breaks free, skittering away on the ground.*

EVE: I can't! I musn't! I won't! *Sexually infuriated, he starts again for her.* I want him! *Adam turns over. Lucifer springs out of her line of sight so that she is looking around at empty space, holding her belly. In short, she has only now awakened in the dream's hangover. Day is dawning.* Where am I? *The baaing of sheep is heard.*

> LUCIFER: The dream ends here, a dark rehearsal of
> the coming day;
> This day you must decide—to crown unreason with
> thy gift of life,
> Or with a tiny death teach justice. *He bends and kisses
> her.*
> I understand thee, woman—I alone.
> Call any time at all.
> *Intimately, pointing into her face:* You know what I
> mean.

Adam sits up. Lucifer goes. Day dawns. Adam stares at Eve, as she sits there. Now she brings her body forward and wipes her eyes.

ADAM: What a night! I don't think I slept five minutes. *She gives him a look.* Did you?

EVE, *after a slight pause, guiltily*: I slept very well, yes.

Disturbed, inward, she gets up, begins gathering pieces of wood for the fire. The baaing of sheep is heard.

ADAM, *looking around*: Say! *She stops moving, looks at him.* The wind! It finally stopped! See? I told you I'd find a place that's not windy!

A blast of howling wind makes them both huddle into their clothes. It dies off. She gets out some figs, places them in a bowl.

EVE: There's your figs.

ADAM: Could it be, you suppose, that everywhere but in Paradise it's just naturally windy? *He bites into a fig.*

EVE: I just don't know, Adam.

ADAM—*he spits out sand*: They're sandy.

EVE: Well, it's windy.

He leans his head on his fist disconsolately.

ADAM: What a way to live! At least if I knew how long it was going to last—

EVE: I still don't understand what's so wrong about digging a hole. We could sit in it and keep out of the wind. Like the groundhogs.

ADAM: I wish you'd stop trying to change the rules! We're not groundhogs. If He meant us to live in holes, He would have given us claws.

EVE: But if He meant us to live in a windstorm He'd have put our eyes in our armpits. *Another blast of wind; then it dies.*

ADAM: Aren't you eating anything?

EVE: I don't feel like it.

ADAM: You know something? You don't look so green today.

EVE, *faintly hopeful, a little surprised at his interest*: I don't?

ADAM: All your color came back. What happened? *He slides over to her, looking quizzically and somewhat excitedly into her face.* You look beautiful, Eve.

EVE—*she laughs nervously*: Well, I can't imagine why!

ADAM, *pushing her back, starting to open her cloak*: It's amazing! I haven't seen you look this way since Paradise! *His hand on her swollen belly stops him.* Oh, excuse me.

EVE, *grasping his hand*: That's all right!

ADAM, *getting up, sliding his hand out of hers*: I forgot that thing. *He stands, looks around.* What a funny morning!

EVE: Why do you always look around like that?

ADAM, *after a slight pause*: I miss God.

EVE, *looking down in sorrow*: I'm sorry, Adam. *Sheep are heard again.*

ADAM, *looking off*: It is just that I'm never really sure what to do next. That grass is giving out; we'll have to move this afternoon.

EVE: I don't think I can walk very far.

ADAM: Goddam clams . . .

EVE: I'm always out of breath, Adam. This thing has gotten very heavy.

ADAM: Does it still move?

EVE: It's doing it now. Would you like to feel it?

ADAM, *touching her belly*: Huh!

EVE: It's almost like a little foot pressing.

ADAM: A foot! No. *He presses his stomach.* I have the same thing sometimes.

EVE, *with sudden hope*: You too? Let me feel it! *She feels his stomach.* I don't feel anything.

ADAM: Well, it stopped. I can't remember—did He say to kill clams before eating?

EVE: But they squash so.

ADAM: I'm not sure we're supposed to eat live things. I can't remember half the things He said any more.

EVE, *tentatively, with some trepidation*: Can I talk to you about that? I'm not sure any more it is those clams.

ADAM: Don't worry, it's the clams. Sits down and eats maybe fifty clams, and suddenly it's not the clams.

EVE: Well, I *like* clams. Especially lately.

ADAM: I like eggs.

EVE: Adam, dear, there's something I feel I should tell you.

ADAM: I had three delicious eggs last—*He breaks off, recalling.* No, no, that was a dream!

EVE, *startled*: You dreamed?

ADAM: Why, did you?

EVE, *quickly*: Tell me yours first.

ADAM: I . . . was in Paradise. Huh! Remember those breakfasts there?

EVE: I wasn't there long enough for breakfast. I was born just before lunch. And I never even got that.

ADAM: Pity you missed it. What a dream! Everything was just the way it used to be. I woke up, and there He was—

EVE: God.

ADAM: Yes. And He brought a tray—and about six beautifully scrambled eggs.

EVE, *with guilt and hunger*: Ohhhh!

ADAM: And no sand whatsoever. I guess it was Sunday because there was also a little tray of warm croissants.

EVE, *sadly charmed*: And then?

ADAM: Same as always—I named a few things. And then we took a nice nap. And angels were playing some soft music. *He hums, trying to recall the tune.* How perfect it all was!

EVE: Until I showed up.

ADAM: Yes. *He looks about with a heightened longing, and, seeing this, she weeps.*

EVE: I don't know why He made me!

ADAM: Well, don't cry, maybe we'll find out some day. I'll round up the sheep. *He starts out.*

EVE—*trying not to call him, she does*: Adam!

ADAM, *halting*: You'll just have to walk. That thing might go away if you get some exercise. *He moves to go.*

EVE: An angel came.

ADAM: When?

EVE: Last night.

ADAM—*happily astounded, he rushes to her*: Which one?

EVE, *fearfully*: It was, ah . . .

ADAM: Chemuel?

EVE: No, not Chemuel.

ADAM: Raphael? Michael?

EVE, *holding her forehead*: No.

ADAM: Well, what'd he look like? Short or tall?

EVE: Quite tall.

ADAM: It wasn't God, was it?

EVE: Oh, not God.

ADAM: What'd he want?

EVE: I—I can't remember it clearly.

ADAM: Was it about getting back into Paradise?

EVE: Well, no. . . .

ADAM: About what we're supposed to do next?

EVE: Not exactly. . . .

ADAM: Why didn't you wake me up?

EVE: I couldn't move!

ADAM: You mean God sends an angel down, and you can't even remember what he said?

EVE: It was about this—*she touches her belly*—thing.

ADAM, *disbelieving; in fact, with disappointment*: About that?

EVE—*she looks up at him*: Would you sit down, Adam? I think I know what we're supposed to do now. *He senses something strange, sits on his heels.* He came through the mist. Like the mist on the sea. Smoke rose from his hair, and his hands smoked.

Lucifer materializes; motionless, he stands in his terrible beauty at the periphery.

ADAM, *with wonder*: Ahhh!

EVE: And he said—*she breaks off in fear as she feels the attraction of the Evil One.*

ADAM: What?

A blast of wind. They huddle. It dies. She has remained staring ahead. Now she turns to him.

EVE: That angel opened my eyes, Adam. I see it all very clearly now—with you the Lord was only somewhat disappointed, but with me He was furious. *Lucifer gravely nods.* And his curse is entirely on me. It is the reason why you've hardly changed out here in the world; but I bleed, and now I am ugly and swollen up like a frog. And I never dream of Paradise, but you do almost every night, and you seem to expect to find it over every hill. And that is right— I think now that you belong in Eden. But not me. And as long as I am with you, you will never find it again. *Slight pause.* Adam, I haven't the power to move from this place, and this is the proof that I must stay here, and you—go back to Paradise.

ADAM, *in conflict with his wishes*: Alone?

EVE: He would lead you there if you walked away alone. You are thirsting for Eden, and the Lord knows that.

ADAM: But so are you.

EVE: Eden is not in me any more.

Lucifer seems to expand with joy.

ADAM: Eve!

EVE: I disgust Him! I am abominable to Him!

ADAM: But the Lord said we are to cleave to one another. I don't think I'm *supposed* to go.

EVE, *bursting into tears, as much with pity for him as with her own indignation:* But you don't like me any more either!

ADAM, *pointing at her belly:* That thing—that thing is what I cannot bear! It turns my stomach! I can't seem to get near you any more! Every time I turn around I'm bumping into it! *She cries louder, turns to find herself face to face with Lucifer.* I don't understand you. Do you *like* that thing?

EVE, *turning back to him from the tempting angel:* I—I don't know!

ADAM: Because if it moves it's alive, and if it's alive we could just hit it! *She gasps, holding her belly.* There, you see? You like it! And this is why I don't know where I am any more! I told you when it started, if you jumped up and down—

EVE: I did jump!

ADAM: You did not jump. You went like that. *He makes a few measly hops.*

EVE: I jumped as hard as I could!

ADAM: I think you're taking *care* of that thing! *Jealously.* You know what's in there, don't you?

EVE, *crying out*: I love thee, husband, and I know this thing will be thy curse!

ADAM: Woman, you will tell me what is in thy belly!

EVE, *clapping her hands over her eyes*: It is a death!

Pause.

ADAM: Whose death?

Pause. Eve lowers her hands, staring ahead.

EVE: Its own.

Pause.

ADAM: Who told thee?

EVE: Lucifer.

ADAM: You're seeing Lucifer again?

EVE: I screamed, but you didn't hear me!

ADAM: Well, I was sleeping!

EVE: You're always sleeping! Every time that son of a bitch comes around, you're someplace else! I would never have touched that apple in the first place if you hadn't left me alone with him!

ADAM: Well, I was *swimming*!

EVE: If you're not swimming, you're sleeping!

ADAM: You mean I can't turn my back for a minute on my own *wife*?

EVE: I couldn't help it, it was like a dream!

ADAM: I don't know how a decent woman can dream about the Devil!

EVE: Adam—he's not all bad.

ADAM: He's not all . . . ! *Light dawns in his head.* Ohhhh! No wonder you looked so juicy when you woke up! I want to know what's so good about him!

EVE, *clapping her hands to her ears*: I can't stand any more!

ADAM, *furiously*: God said I am thy master, woman, and you are going to tell me what went on here! No wonder I haven't been able to get near you. There's been something strange about you for months!

EVE: There is a man in my belly, Adam.

ADAM, *chilled with astonishment, wonder, fear*: A man!

EVE: He told me.

Long pause.

ADAM: How could a man fit in there?

EVE: Well . . . small. To start off with. Like the baby monkeys and the little zebras—

ADAM: Zebras! He's got you turning us into animals now? No human being has ever been born except grown up! I may be confused about a lot of things, but I know facts!

EVE: But it's what God said—we were to go forth and multiply.

ADAM, *striking his chest indignantly*: If we're going to multiply, it'll be through me! Same as it always was! What am I going to do with you? After everything he did to us with his goddamned lies, you still—

EVE: Husband, he told me to do with it exactly what you have told me to do with it.

ADAM, *struck*: What I . . . ?

EVE: He told me it is a man and he told me to kill it. What the Devil hath spoken, thou hast likewise spoken.

Silence. Neither moves. One sheep baas, like a sinister snarl. A sudden surge of wind, which quickly dies.

ADAM, *tortured*: But I had no idea it was a man when I said that.

EVE, *holding her belly, with a long gaze beyond them both*: Adam . . . I believe I am meant to bring out this man—alone.

ADAM, *furiously, yet unable to face her directly*: Are you putting me with that monster?

EVE: But why do you all want him dead!

ADAM: I forbid you to say that again! I am not Lucifer! *A heartbroken cry escapes him.* Eve! *He sinks to his knees. He curls up in ignominy, then prostrates himself before her, flat out on the ground, pressing his lips to her foot.* Forgive me! *He weeps. Wind blasts. It dies.*

EVE—*a new thought interrupts her far-off gaze, and she looks at his prostrate body*: Will you dig us a hole?

ADAM—*he joyously scrambles up and kisses her hand*: A hole!

EVE: It needn't be too big—

ADAM: What do you mean? I'll dig you the biggest hole you ever saw in your life! Woman . . . *With a cry of gratitude he sweeps her into his arms.* Woman, thou art my salvation!

EVE: Oh, my darling, that's so good to hear!

ADAM: How I thirst for thee! My doe, my rabbit . . .

EVE: My five-pointed buck, my thundering bull!

ADAM, *covering his crotch*: Oh, Eve, thy forgiveness hath swelled me like a ripened ear of corn.

EVE: Oh, how sweet. Then I will forgive thee endlessly.

Lucifer shows alarm and rising anger.

ADAM: Say, now, the Lord will probably expect me to think of a name for him. Or do you want to? *He indicates her belly.*

EVE: No, you. You're so good at names.

ADAM— *he thinks, paces*: Well, let's see . . .

EVE: I'll be quiet. *She watches him with pleasure.* It ought to be something clear and clean and—something for a *handsome* man.

ADAM: Y'know, when I saw the first giraffe—it may not fit, but it went through my mind at the time.

EVE: What?

ADAM: Frank?

EVE: Don't you think that's a little too, ah . . . ?

ADAM: I guess so, yes. Maybe it ought to begin with A.

EVE, *simultaneously*: . . . *to begin with an A.*

 They point at each other and laugh.

ADAM: I mean because he's the first.

EVE: He's the first.

 They laugh again.

EVE: Isn't it marvelous that we both have the same thoughts . . .

ADAM: Both have the same thoughts.

EVE, *in the clear*: . . . again!

ADAM, *lifting his arms thankfully*: What a God we have!

EVE: How perfectly excellent is the Lord!

Lucifer throws up his hands and goes into darkness, holding his head.

ADAM, *suddenly looking down at the ground, astonished*: Eve?

EVE: What, my darling?

ADAM: Is this grass growing?

EVE, *looking about quickly at the ground*: I believe it is!

ADAM, *looking front*: Look at the pasture! It's up to their bellies!

EVE: Adam, the wind . . . !

They look up and around. There is silence.

ADAM: Woman, we must have done something right! *He looks upward.* I think He loves us again.

EVE—*her hands shoot up, open-palmed, her eyes wide with terror*: Sssh!

ADAM: Could it possibly be . . .

EVE, *a hand moving toward her belly*: Ssh, sh!

ADAM: . . . that the curse is *over? She grips her belly. She suddenly rushes right and is stopped by a wild, curling cry of a high-screaming French horn. He is oblivious to the sound.* What are you doing? *She turns and rushes upstage; he is starting after her, and she is stopped short by a whining blow on a timpani and a simultaneous snarling trumpet blast. He nearly catches her, but she gets away and is rushing left and is stopped by a pair of cacophonic flutes. He catches her now.* Eve! *She wrenches free of him—and she shows terror of him; and for an instant they are two yards apart, he uncomprehending, she in deadly fear of him. Protesting*: It's Adam. I am thy husband!

She rushes to a point and halts, crying upwards.

EVE: *Chemuuuuu-elllll!* Merciful sweet angel, take me out of myself! *She is seized by her agony and rolls over and over along the ground, as a massive cacophonic music flares up. Adam is put off, unmanned, afraid to touch her. She slams her hands on the ground as she writhes on her back.* God! Oh, God!

ADAM: Maybe it'll get better.

EVE: It will get worse. And when it gets worse it—*she sits up, recalling*—will get perfectly worse. . . . *A contrac-*

tion. Oh, God! *Stretching on her side, hands outstretched*: I call on any angel whatsoever!

ADAM, *calling upward*: Chemuel, come! Bring mercy!

EVE: Help me, demon! Come to me, Lucifer!

ADAM, *clapping his ears shut*: Aiiiii!

EVE, *as though whipped, submissively begging*: Take out this agony! Demon, I am awake! Still me, angel! Take him out of my flesh!

ADAM, *falling to his knees*: God in Heaven, she is out of her mind!

EVE: I am *in* my mind—He never gave me a chance!

ADAM: Lord, give her a chance!

EVE: No, He loves this! God, if this is Thy pleasure, then I owe Thee nothing any more, and I call, I call, I call for— *A seizure; with each call she pounds the earth.* God. Oh, God. Oh, God. God—damn—you—God!

ADAM, *curled up in terror*: Aiiii!

Lucifer appears at the periphery.

EVE: Still me, demon . . . take this out! Don't waste another minute! Not a minute more! He is bursting me! Kill him! Kill him!

Lucifer takes a step toward her and is halted by trumpets: a single melodious chord. She faints. Adam tries to rise and, seeing her, he faints too. God enters. A step behind Him are Azrael, Angel of Death, and Chemuel, Angel of Mercy.

GOD, *standing over her, looking down*: Now bend, Azrael,

and blow thy cold death across her lip. *Azrael bends and exhales over her face. Eve shudders as with icy cold and gasps in air, still asleep.* That's enough. Chemuel, in thy compassion, drive anguish to the corner of her mind, and seal it up. *Chemuel kneels, kisses her once. Eve exhales with relief. God walks a few yards away and sits.* Go away, Death. *Azrael stands fast.* Go, Azrael. And wait her need. *Azrael exits unwillingly.* Chemuel, in thy mercy, deliver Eve. *Chemuel reaches, lays his hand on her swollen belly, and with a short pull removes the swelling; clutching it to his breast, he starts to lean to kiss her again.* That's enough. *Chemuel hesitates, glancing up at God.* Go, Chemuel, and wait her need. *Chemuel stands and goes out.* Now in thy slumber let us reason together. *Adam and Eve sit up, their eyes shut in sleep.* Behold the stranger thine agony hath made. *A youth of sixteen appears, his eyes shut, his arms drawn in close to his body, his hands clasping his forward-tilted head. He moves waywardly, like a windblown leaf, and as he at last approaches Eve, he halts some feet away as God speaks again.* Here is the first life of thy life; woman. And it is fitting that the first letter stand before his name. But seeing that in thy extremity thou hast already offered his life to Lucifer; and seeing, Adam, that in your ignorance you have likewise threatened him with murder— *He loses his calm*—all of which amazes Me and sets My teeth on edge—*He breaks off, gritting His teeth*—I am nevertheless mindful that this child—*He turns to the youth* —is innocent. So we shall try again. And rather than call him Abel, who was in jeopardy, he shall be Cain, for his life's sake. *He stands.* Now Cain is born!

Cain lies down, coiled beside Eve. She sits up, opens her eyes, and looks down at Cain.

EVE, *joyfully surprised*: Ahhh!

ADAM, *walking quickly, seeing Cain*: What's that?

EVE: It is . . .

GOD: Cain. Thy son.

Both gasp, surprised by His presence.

EVE—*she suddenly feels her flat belly and with a cry prostrates before God*: I see I have been favored of Thee, O Lord!

GOD, *indicating the inert Cain:* Here is thine innocence returned to thee, which thou so lightly cast away in Eden. Now protect him from the worm of thine own evil, which this day hath uncovered in thee. Look in My face, woman.

EVE, *covering her eyes*: I dare not, for I doubted Thy goodness!

GOD: And will you doubt Me any more?

EVE: Never, never, never!

GOD: Then lift up thine eyes.

She slowly dares to face Him on her knees.

EVE: I have gotten a man from the Lord.

GOD: Thou art the mother of mankind.

EVE: And generations unknown to me shall spring from my loins. *He extends His hand. She rests hers on it and rises.*

> I am the river abounding in fish,
> I am the summer sun arousing the bee,
> As the rising moon is held in her place

By Thine everlasting mind, so am I held
In Thine esteem.

GOD: Eve, you are my favorite girl!

*An angelic waltz strikes up. God sweeps Eve in a glorious
dance all over the stage. Adam, happiness on his face,
makes light and abortive attempts to cut in. God and Eve
exit, dancing, Adam trailing behind and calling.*

ADAM: Eve! Look at Him dance! *Laughing, bursting with
joy, he waltzes out after them.*

*Lucifer, alone with Cain coiled up nearby, looks off toward
the party and shakes his head.*

LUCIFER: You've got to hand it to Him. *He turns front,
staring.* What a system! *Now he looks down at Cain.* So
this is Cain. *He crouches over Cain.* With the kiss of
Lucifer begin thy life; let my nature coil around thine
own. And on thy shoulders may I climb the throne. *He
bends and kisses him.*

CURTAIN

Act III

The family discovered asleep. A primitive shelter is suggested, hanging skins, and a cooking area in one corner. God is seated on a rock. He is thoughtfully watching them. He shakes his head, baffled, then raises a hand.

GOD: Azrael! *Azrael lights up behind the left screen.* Angel of Death, I have work for you today. The time has come when the human race will spread across the earth. But these people have all but forgotten God. They eat to live and live to eat. By what law shall the multitudes be governed when even now my name is hardly mentioned any more? *Stands, looking down at the people.* Therefore, when this dawn comes, you will blow visions of death into their dreams. But be careful not to kill anybody; you are only to remind them that they cannot live forever. And having seen death, I hope they'll think of God again, and begin to face their terrible responsibilities. *Azrael starts to raise his arms.* Not yet!—wait till dawn. I want them to remember what they've dreamed when they awake. *To the people*: Dear people, I shall be watching every move you make today. *He exits. Lucifer comes up out of the trap. Looks about, notices a golden bowl and picks it up.*

LUCIFER: Every time I come up here they've got more

junk. What a race—a little prosperity and they don't even need the Devil.

EVE, *awakening*: What spirit art thou?

LUCIFER: It's me, honey.

EVE: Why don't you just go to hell and stay there?

LUCIFER: Darling, I'm terribly worried about your soul! A beautiful, intelligent woman like you can't waste her life just cooking and doing the house. You simply have no idea what you're missing!

EVE: I have absolutely everything I ever dreamed of, Angel. . . .

LUCIFER: But don't you want to broaden your horizons?

EVE: No! *She lies back down.*

LUCIFER: Whatever you say, darling. Sweet dreams, pretty girl. *Comes away from her.* For all the bad I've done I might as well have stayed in heaven. Only bad trouble will make them call to me for help. I'll break them apart!—or they'll turn the whole earth into this smug suburb of heaven. Now let's see—Cain is jealous of his brother; suppose we start from there. . . . *He leaps to Cain when the light of dawn glows and Azrael appears behind the screen. Lucifer hides to observe him. Sotto.* Azrael? What's this about? *Azrael raises his caped arms menacingly.* My God, is somebody going to die? *Azrael blows three loud, short breaths. The people instantly groan. Azrael vanishes. Lucifer comes down to the people.* Groaning! Did he blow dreams into them?

ADAM—*sits up*: What a dream! *She turns to him expect-antly.* I think I saw . . . something die.

EVE, *against her fear*: Maybe a sheep.

ADAM: No. It had a face.

LUCIFER: But none of them is old or sick—how do they die?

EVE: A person's face?

ADAM: Yes. And there was blood.

EVE: Blood!

LUCIFER: Blood?—Is he setting them up for a murder?— Of course! What better way to make them guilty and put the fear of God back into them! What a mistake I nearly made—I've got to keep them out of trouble, not get them into it.

CAIN, *sitting up*: What a dream!

ADAM and EVE: What!

CAIN: I think I saw something die.

LUCIFER: And here's my opening at last! I'll stop this killing and they'll love me for it, and hate the Lord who has to have a death and their remorse! Oh, this is beautiful! But which one kills, and who's supposed to die? *He continuously moves around the periphery and sometimes in among them, searchingly, awaiting his opening.*

ABEL, *sitting up*: What a dream!

ADAM: That's enough. Eve, make breakfast.

ABEL: I was flying across the sky. . . .

EVE: But that's a wonderful dream!

ABEL: And then I fell. . . . *Mystified*: And an angel kissed me.

CAIN, *instantly—an exhale of recognition, his finger raised:* Ohhhhh! *All turn to him as he points to Abel.* I remember now. He died. *Eve gasps.*

EVE: Don't say that! *She gets up and goes to Abel and, holding his head in her arms, kisses him. Adam moves her aside, and he kisses him.*

LUCIFER: It's Abel dies? But who kills him?

CAIN, *kisses Abel:* I saw thee on the ground, thy face crushed, and a blood-covered flail . . . rolling away.

ADAM: All right, now wait a minute.

CAIN, *turning to Adam:* How is it that he dies in my sleep? *Turning to Abel:* You haven't done anything, have you?

ABEL, *to Eve:* The minute anything happens he always blames me!

EVE: You two stop fighting.

ADAM: Now pay attention. Nobody ever dreamed of death before, so I don't want to hear any arguments of any kind whatsoever today.

LUCIFER: Good man! *To Eve:* Brighten it up.

EVE: I'll make a nice breakfast!

CAIN: Father. *Adam turns to him, sensing his strange intensity.* When you decided to leave Paradise, did God . . . ?

EVE: What's Paradise got to do with this?

CAIN: I wish we could talk about it, Mother! Didn't God give you any instructions when you left? I mean, how do we know we're saying the right prayers. Or maybe we don't pray enough.

ADAM: Oh, no. I'm sure He'd let us know if we were doing something wrong.

CAIN: But maybe that's what the dream was for.

ADAM, *struck by this*: Say!

CAIN: Because lately when I'm out in the fields chopping weeds—it suddenly seems so strange . . .

EVE, *impatiently*: What, dear?

CAIN: Did God order you to make me the farmer and Abel to tend the sheep?

ADAM: You can't expect Him to go into those kind of details, Cain. He just felt it was time we went out in the world and multiplied, that's all.

CAIN: Father, I've never understood why you couldn't have stayed in the Garden and multiplied.

EVE: In the *Garden*!

ADAM: Oh, no, boy—

EVE: That's not something you do in the *Garden,* darling.

CAIN: Well, what did He say, exactly, when you left?

ADAM: He said to get out—

EVE: Not "Get out!"

ADAM, *quickly*: No, not "Get out!"

EVE: I think he's overtired.

CAIN: I am not overtired! Why do you always make everything ridiculous? I'm not talking about sheep or farming; I'm talking about what God wants us to *do*!

ABEL: If you think He wants me to farm, I'll be glad to switch.

CAIN, *to Adam with a laugh*: He's going to farm!

ADAM, *laughing*: God help us!

ABEL, *protesting*: Why!

CAIN: With your sense of responsibility, we'd be eating thistle soup!

EVE, *touching Abel*: He's just more imaginative.

LUCIFER: Will you just shut up?

CAIN: Imaginative!

ABEL: Have I ever lost a sheep?

CAIN: How *could* you lose them? They always end up in my corn.

ABEL: Cain, that only happened once!

CAIN, *with raw indignation*: Go out there and sweat the way I do and tell me it only happened once!

EVE: He's just younger!

CAIN: And I'm older, and I'll be damned if I plant another crop until he fences those sheep!

LUCIFER: Stop this!

EVE, *to Adam*: Stop this!

CAIN: Why must you always take his side?

EVE: But how can he build a fence?

CAIN: The same way I plant a crop, Mother! By bending his back! Abel, I'm warning you, if you ever again—

ADAM: Boys, boys!

ABEL, *turning away*: If he wants a fence, I think he should build it.

CAIN: *I* should build it! Are the corn eating the sheep or the sheep eating the corn?

ABEL: It's not natural for me to build a fence.

CAIN: Not natural! You've been talking to God lately?

ABEL: I don't know anything about God. But it's the nature of sheep to move around, and it's the nature of corn to stay in one place. So the fence should fence the thing that stays in one place and not the thing that moves around.

ADAM: That's logical, Cain.

CAIN: In other words, the work belongs to me and the whole wide world belongs to him!

ADAM, *at a loss*: No, that's not fair either.

ABEL, *angering, to Adam*: Well, I can't fence the mountains, can I? I can't fence the rivers where they go to drink. *To Cain*: I know you work harder, Cain, but I didn't decide that. I've even thought sometimes that it is unfair, and maybe we should change places for a while—

CAIN: You wouldn't last a week.

ABEL, *crying out*: Then what am I supposed to do? *Cain is close, staring into his face, a tortured expression in his eyes which puzzles Abel.* Why is he looking like that? *Suddenly Cain embraces Abel, hugging him close.*

ADAM: Attaboy!

EVE, *puzzled and alarmed*: Cain?

CAIN—*he lets Abel go and moves a few steps, staring*: I don't know what's happening to me.

ADAM: Abel, shake his hand. Go on, make up. You're both sorry.

ABEL, *holding out his hand*: Cain?

LUCIFER, *victoriously to Heaven*: Why don't you give up?

Cain has just raised his hand to approach Abel when a large snake is dropped in their midst from Heaven. Eve screams. Lucifer rushes and flings it out of sight.

LUCIFER: Scat! Get out of here!

EVE: It flew in and flew out!

ADAM: A flying snake?

Instantly the high howling of several coyotes is heard, and the family turns in all directions, as though toward an invading force.

LUCIFER, *off to one side, looking up to Heaven*: Father, this is *low*!

ADAM, *looking about at the air*: Something is happening. *To Eve, who is staring about*: I think . . . I'd better tell them. *She covers her eyes in trepidation.* Eve? Maybe we're supposed to, now.

EVE, *lowering her hands*: All right. Then maybe everything will be as it was again.

ADAM: Boys? Maybe you'd better sit down, boys.

ABEL: Tell what, Pa?

They all sit except Eve, who remains standing, staring about apprehensively.

ADAM: About the question of leaving Paradise—I don't want you to think that we tried to mislead you or anything like that.

EVE, *pleadingly to Cain*: It's just everything was going so good, you see?

ADAM, *with a glance around at the air*: But it looks like something is happening, so maybe we better get this settled.

ABEL: What, Pa?

ADAM: We . . . didn't exactly *decide* to go, y'see. We were ah—*he blinks away a tear*—told to leave.

CAIN: *Told?*

ABEL: Why, Pa?

ADAM, *fumbling*: Why? Well . . . *He turns helplessly to Eve.* Why?

EVE: We just didn't fit in, you see. I mean if a person doesn't fit in—

ADAM: If we're going to tell it, we better tell it.

EVE: But the way you're telling it, it sounds like it was all my fault!

ADAM: I didn't say anything yet!

EVE: Well, when are you going to say it?

ADAM, *setting himself*: Well—as we told you before, I was alone with God for a long time, and then—

ABEL: He made Mama.

ADAM: Right.

ABEL, *with a big smile*: And you liked her right away, heh?

CAIN: Of course he did.

ADAM: She was gorgeous. Of course, there wasn't much choice. *He laughs.*

EVE: Ha. Ha. Ha.

ADAM: Well, anyway, I believe I mentioned there was this tree—with an apple—

ABEL: Of good and evil.

ADAM: Right.

CAIN: Which you're never allowed to eat under any circumstances.

ADAM: Right. Well, the thing is, you see—we ate it.

ABEL—*thrilled and scared, he laughs*: You ate it!

CAIN: I thought you said you—

ADAM: No, we ate it.

ABEL, *more scared now*: Not Mama, though.

ADAM: Mama too.

*Cain goes to a lyre and, turning his back on them, he plays.
They watch him for a moment, aware of his intense feeling.*

ABEL, *avidly*: And then what happened?

Cain strums as loud as he can, then stops.

ADAM, *with a worried glance at Cain*: Well, the next thing
—I looked at her, y'see. And there was something funny.
I didn't know what it was. And then I realized. She was
naked.

Cain now turns to them.

CAIN AND ABEL: Mama?

EVE: Well, *he* was too.

CAIN—*shocked, he drops the lyre*: Mama!

LUCIFER, *holding his head*: Ohhh!

EVE: We didn't know it, darling!

CAIN: How could you not know you were naked?

EVE: Well, we were like children; like you, like Abel. You
remember, when Abel was a baby and ran around—

CAIN, *outraged, accusing*: But you weren't a baby!

EVE, *to Adam, at a loss*: Aren't you going to say anything?

ABEL, *explaining for Adam*: Well, they were like animals.

CAIN, *pained, horrified*: Don't you say a thing like that!

ADAM, *to Cain*: Well, I told you—I could smell water?

ABEL: Sure! And they could hear the trout talking.

CAIN: But you never said you were actually . . . *animals.*

ADAM: Now just a minute, Cain. That was the way God wanted it—

CAIN: I can't believe that! God could never have wanted my mother going around without any clothes on!

ADAM, *angrily, standing*: You mean *I* wouldn't let her put her clothes on?

EVE, *going to him*: Darling, we were innocent!

CAIN, *furiously*: You were naked and innocent? Don't you understand that that's why he threw you out?

EVE: But He loved us most when we were naked. He only got mad when we knew we were. *Slight pause.*

CAIN, *swept by this truth*: No wonder we dreamed of death!

EVE: Why?

CAIN: We've been saying all the wrong prayers. We shouldn't be thanking God—we should be begging His forgiveness. We've been living as though we were innocent. We've been living as though we were blessed!

EVE: But we are, darling.

CAIN: We are cursed, Mother!

EVE, *furiously to Adam*: You should never have told him!

CAIN: Why did you lie to us?

ADAM: Now just a minute . . .

CAIN, *accusingly*: I always *knew* there was something you weren't saying!

ADAM: Just a minute! *Slight pause.* We didn't want to frighten you, that's all. But maybe now you're old enough to understand.—He did curse us when He threw us out. And part of the curse is that we will have to die.

CAIN: *We're* going to die?

ABEL: Like the sheep, you mean?

ADAM: Sheep, birds, everything.

CAIN: You and Mama, too? You mean we wouldn't see you any more?

EVE: Don't worry about it, darling, I'm sure we have a long, long time yet.

CAIN: You mean before He got angry you would never die?

ADAM: Far as I know—yes.

CAIN: Oh, my God—then He must have been absolutely furious with you.

EVE: I'm sure He's forgiven us, dear, or we wouldn't have you and everything so wonderful—

CAIN, *sinking to his knees*: Listen to me! I tell you we have been warned. Now we must do what has never been done.

EVE: Do what?

CAIN: We must give this day—not to the animals or the crops; this day we must give to God. I tell you—*he looks upward tenderly*—if we will open up our sins to Him and cleanse ourselves, he might show his face and tell us we are supposed to live. Father, Mother, Abel—come and pray with me.

ADAM, *to Eve*: Well—a prayer wouldn't hurt.

EVE, *recalling*: Maybe he's right. Maybe it'll all be sweet again. *Going to her knees*: What should we pray, darling?

Cain, faces Heaven. Adam goes to his knees. And finally Abel.

CAIN: Almighty God, seeing that our parents were thrown out of Paradise for their transgressions against Thee, we, Cain and Abel, beseech Thy forgiveness. Let this family live, let us be innocent again! Now each one, give up the sin.

Adam and Eve shut their eyes and concentrate. Abel watches them, then leans over to Eve.

ABEL, *with a glance at the praying Cain*: Does this mean I'm building a fence?

CAIN, *eyes shut*: It seems to me that when a person dies in his brother's dream he ought to pray!

ADAM: I saw it too, Abel—you were dead. I think you'd better pray.

Pause. All heads are lowered. Lucifer stands up. He comes down to them and sits next to Abel.

ABEL, *softly*: Mother!

EVE: Sssh!

ABEL: Someone has come.

ADAM: I don't see anybody.

A slight pause. They contemplate, but Abel is glancing apprehensively toward Lucifer.

ABEL: Who art thou?

The family turns quickly to him, astonished, Lucifer being invisible to all but Abel.

LUCIFER: I am what you fear in your heart is true—your brother is dangerous. Tell him you'll build the fence. *Abel reacts in refusal.* This man is inconsolable!

ABEL: Why?

LUCIFER: She loves you best, Abel.

ABEL: But Cain is loved!

EVE: How sweet! *To Adam:* Did you hear?

LUCIFER: Cain has her respect, but her love has gone to you. Tell him you'll build it if you care to live! This man is murderous! *Now Abel turns with new eyes to Cain.*

ABEL: About the fence—

CAIN: Yes?

ABEL: You're right. It's not the corn that eat the sheep but the sheep that eat the corn—

LUCIFER: Attaboy!

EVE, *to Adam, happily*: Listen!

ABEL: So I will build the fence around the sheep.

EVE, *to Adam*: Do you hear!

ADAM: Marvelous.

CAIN: Where would you build it?

ABEL: Well—anywhere out of the way. In the valley?

CAIN: I need the valley.

ABEL: Oh . . . On the hillside?

CAIN: I'll need the hillside. I'm planning to set out quite a large vineyard this spring.

ABEL: Where would you suggest, then?

CAIN: There is very rich pasture across the mountain.

ABEL: That's . . . pretty far away, though, isn't it?

CAIN: I don't think it's all that far.

LUCIFER: Agree! Agree!

ABEL, *swallowing his resentment*: All right, Cain.

LUCIFER: I know how you feel, son, but lying is better than dying.

EVE, *affected by Abel's anguish*: Cain, dear, I want you to tell him you didn't mean that before—

LUCIFER: Abel, shut her up—

EVE, *to Cain, insistently*: You won't make him go so far away to pasture, will you?

LUCIFER: She is killing you, word by loving word!

ABEL: I don't mind, Mother. In fact—

LUCIFER: I *like* long walks.

ABEL: I *like* long walks.

EVE: But you *agreed* to build the fence! *To Cain*: Why must you humiliate him?

Cain slams his hands down on the ground and springs up furiously, goes to a big rock and picks it up.

LUCIFER, *to Abel*: Watch out! Don't turn your back on him! *Abel quickly turns to watch his brother.*

EVE: What are you doing?

Cain places the boulder on top of another.

CAIN: What has never been done. It has come to me to make an offering to the Lord.

LUCIFER, *shaking a fist at Heaven*: Don't you ever give up?

EVE, *vastly relieved*: That's a wonderful idea!

ADAM: Say, now! That sounds very good, Cain.

EVE: You think He'll come?

ADAM: He might. The way Cain loves Him, He might just stop by. *To Cain, with his expertise*: Take the best of thy corn and the first of thy wheat, and a little parsley—He always rather liked parsley.

Cain finds a flat stone and sets it on top of the altar he is constructing. Eve immediately takes a broom and starts sweeping the area.

EVE: What about some grapes?

ADAM, *calling to Cain*: Grapes too!

CAIN: The grapes aren't too good this year—

EVE: You'd better not, then.

ADAM, *all excited*: Don't listen to her; it doesn't matter if they're not too good, it's the feeling behind it. Because

He's fair, Cain, you'll see. And here's another thing. We've got to praise Him more. We haven't been praising Him enough.

EVE: Praise God! Praise the Lord!

ADAM: Will you wait! *To Cain*: Hurry up, get the stuff. *Cain rushes back to load a tray with his crops.*

EVE, *clasping her hands together feverishly*: He's going to come! I feel it, I tell you I feel it!

ADAM, *supervising Cain, calling*: I'd throw in a few onions. *To Eve:* Loved a good onion.

EVE: It's going to be like it was again! *She rushes to Abel.* Push back your hair, darling. Adam, there's dirt on your cheek. *Adam brushes it off. Abel fixes his hair. Cain turns to them now with a tray loaded with vegetables and fruit. Silence for an instant; then Eve suddenly is swept forward to him.* Would you mind, darling? *She picks an apple off the tray.* No apples. *She hides the apple in her clothes.*

CAIN, *in tension*: Is it all right, Pa?

Adam comes forward, inspects the tray. Silence.

ADAM: This looks absolutely beautiful, Cain. Now, when you see His face, regard the right eye. Because that's the one He loves you with. The left one squints, y'see, because that's the one He judges with. So watch the right eye and don't be frightened.

CAIN: I love Him, Father.

ADAM: I know that, Cain, and now you will know His love for thee. *He kisses Cain, who turns and tensely starts for the altar.*

EVE: Cain!

He halts. She comes to him, elevated within. She kisses the offering. Then she kisses him. He turns again to the altar. Abel steps before him. They stare at one another. Now Cain leans and kisses him. Then he carefully sets the offering on the altar and steps back. All go to their knees before the altar, as—

EVE, *to Adam, tentatively*: I think Abel ought to make an offering too.

Abel sits up, and Adam considers this. Cain remains bowed. Lucifer cries out, rushing about before Abel.

LUCIFER: Don't! Under no circumstances must you get into this competition!

CAIN: It was my idea, Mother. Can't he do it another time?

EVE: It was just a suggestion. You don't have to get angry.

ABEL, *struck by his vision*: Maybe He would come because of me. . . .

LUCIFER: What are *you* guilty about? Just because your mother loves you best? Lie back and enjoy it.

ABEL: But it is not fair to Cain, and I can't bear that any more! I want God to bring us peace!

LUCIFER: And what if it turns out God also loves you best? Is *that* fair to Cain?

ABEL: But—Cain would have to accept *that!*

LUCIFER: Boy, even with God's help, nobody can be Number One and good at the same time. Don't compete!

ABEL: Get thee behind me! *He draws his knife and rushes upstage.*

EVE, *to Adam*: He's going to do it! *Calling to Abel, who is exiting*: Pick a nice fat lamb, darling!

LUCIFER, *as he rushes upstage after Abel*: Abel! Don't call down God!

Cain is still on his knees, staring ahead. Eve feels his anguish.

EVE: He'll come now, dear, and He'll bless you both, as I do. *But Cain refuses to turn to her; she sees his hurt.* I love thee, Cain, I always loved thee from the hour of thy conception!

LUCIFER, *looks to Heaven*: What a genius that old fart is—with one dream of death he's got them all guilty! By God, I'll free them now or never—with the truth! *He exits.*

Abel enters, holding before him a slab of wood loaded with the flesh and entrails of a lamb, his hands dripping blood. Adam instantly goes to him, smears his own hand, and snaps the blood into the air toward the sky.

ADAM: The blood is the life, and the life is the Lord's.

EVE—*she looks up to the sky*:

> Now, Maker, show Thyself and spread Thy peace
> On all of us, my Abel and my Cain.

She and Adam kiss Abel from his right and left. He sets his offering on the altar. The deep bellow of a bull is heard.

ALL: Aiee!

The bellowing resounds again, and now a figure rises behind the altar, a man with the head of a bull. At the sight they all prostrate themselves on the ground.

LUCIFER: A second time I come with thine awakening,
    Mankind!
Nobody's guilty any more!
And for your progeny now and forever
I declare one massive, eternal, continuous parole!
From here on out there is no sin or innocence
But only Man. *He flings off his mask.*
Now claim thy birthright! *He leaps, stands away from
    the altar, welcoming arms outflung.*
Total freedom!

EVE, *leaps up*: Thank God!

ADAM, *springing to his feet*: That's the Devil!

LUCIFER: There are two Gods, Adam—in Heaven, God;
and God on earth is me!

ADAM: Slaughter him! *He starts for Lucifer, and the boys
stand. Eve throws herself before Lucifer to shield him.*
Woman!

EVE: I believe this angel!

ADAM: This is the enemy!

EVE: I won't deny it any more—this spirit makes me
happy!

ADAM, *to the altar*: Lord, show thy face, my wife is going
to Hell!

EVE: Adam! *She raises her hand gently toward him.*

> Where has all our old contentment gone?
> You were so long in Paradise
> With God, that all your dreams go there,
> But the only home I ever had is on this dust,
> This windy world,
> And here I am condemned. I know God rules in
>   Heaven,
> But in the name of peace, I have to speak the truth:
> Except for one short dance—*she nearly weeps*—
> God never showed me any kindness.

ADAM: Woman!

> EVE: I see it, husband!
> This God is mine—I know it!
> For only this one frees me of my sin.

ADAM: There is one God!

EVE: No—two! One for me and one for—*A strange light blossoms around the altar, and, seeing it, she breaks off and like the others backs away. Lucifer rushes down to her.*

LUCIFER: Let's end this war! Dance with me, woman. Show God your love and end this stupid war!

A wild music explodes, then diminishes as Lucifer pulls her to himself, and in conflict she breaks and with arms spread calls to Abel.

EVE: Abel! Cain! *Rushing to them, grabbing them:* Love! Love, my darlings!

ADAM: I forbid this! God's coming!

EVE—*clamping both their heads to her, she calls out to Adam and Heaven*: Is God not pleased if peace comes in? *She springs from them and then turns back invitingly to them.* Let hate go out and love come in!

> LUCIFER: Now save yourselves with music and the truth!
> Be what you are and as you are.
> Give God to Adam, boys—and I will give you Eve!

The music flies up: Eve begins to dance—awkwardly at first, and Lucifer grabs her, awakens her again, and her body loosens, writhes; then she flies to Abel, who is embarrassed but quickly learns, and now she flies to Cain, who is stiff at first, but Lucifer helps him loosen up, and finally she is whirling among the three of them, kissing them in turn, her hands flowing over their bodies and theirs over hers—and suddenly Cain explodes into a prancing step, flapping his arms like a giant mating bird. Eve is astonished, innocently laughs, but in a swoop he pulls her down and climbs onto her. The truth is out—fuck her, Cain, and save the world! *Adam rushes to separate them. Lucifer grabs him.* Shame! How can you be so selfish! *And with Cain on his stunned but compliant mother and Abel trying to hold out till Cain is done—God appears behind the altar.*

Adam roars a gigantic, horrified roar. Silence. Cain rolls off Eve and sits looking up at the Presence. Eve sits up. Adam prostrates himself.

ADAM: Glory to God in the highest!

LUCIFER: Good morning, sir. *With an ironic gesture toward the crew*: May I introduce you to mankind? I don't believe

I need labor the point—to the naked eye how pious and God-fearing they were; but with a moment's instruction and the right kind of music, a bear would blush at their morality. Dear Father, what are we fighting about? Truly, Lord, what is Man beyond his appetite? *Extends his hand.* Come, make peace; share Heaven—I the God of what-they-are, and you in charge of their improvement. In you let them find their hopes, in me their pleasure, and shut the gates of Hell forever. Sir, I am ready to take my place.

Striving against anger, God turns his head to each of the people in turn. Then He looks down at the offerings and picks out an onion.

GOD: Peace, children, on this first Sabbath. Whose is this?

LUCIFER: You'll accept those offerings when the filth in their hearts stinks to Heaven!

GOD: Whose is this?

CAIN, *with uncertainty*: That was mine, Lord.

GOD: Do you want me to taste it?

LUCIFER: You saw him on his mother!

GOD: Cain?

CAIN, *his eyes averted*: If it please Thee.

GOD: Why?

CAIN: It's . . . my *onion,* sir.

GOD: Then you still have respect for an onion?

CAIN: Lord, it's my work, my labor; it is the best of all I've made.

GOD, *with angry eyes*: And were you not the best that I had made?

Cain looks up, aware, and lowers his eyes in shame. God bites the onion, chews it.

GOD: That . . . is a good onion, Cain. *Cain falls to his knees weeping.* And this is Abel's meat?

ABEL: It's mine, sir, yes.

GOD: Mutton.

EVE: Ah, no, sir—lamb.

GOD—*He glances at her, then with high interest leans and inhales the delicious scent*: Ohhh, yes.

ABEL, *encouraged*: My youngest, fattest lamb, Lord. I hope it will please Thee.

EVE: I usually sprinkle it with salt and pepper first. . . .

GOD: You might try rubbing a bud of garlic over it.

EVE: Oh, I will!

ADAM: Do that next time, definitely.

EVE: Oh, Yes, Adam!

Now God picks up a piece of meat. All grow tense. Abel raises his head to watch. God puts the meat in His mouth and chews, His eyes opening wider with the taste.

GOD: What in the world do you feed your flock?

ABEL, *joyously*: I find the sweetest grass, sir!

CAIN: And corn. *God turns to him. Abel, tense, turns to him.*

GOD, *understanding*: Oh, yes. I see. *He turns slowly to Abel.* Abel? Rise. *Abel springs to his feet.* Young man, this is undoubtedly the sweetest, most delicious, delicate, and profoundly *satisfying* piece of meat I have ever tasted since the world began.

Adam, filled with glory, comes to Abel and shakes his hand.

ADAM: Boy, this is our proudest moment.

EVE—*unable to hold back, she starts for Abel*: Darling! *She grabs Abel's face, kisses him on the lips, and turns up to God.* There is one God now and forever, there is no other on earth or in Heaven!

GOD: And don't you forget it, either. *Turning to Lucifer, who is staring at the ground*: I seem to have forgotten what you were saying. What was that all about, fallen angel?

LUCIFER, *bitterly*: About the truth, sir—my mistake. But this isn't over yet!

GOD, *steps down from the altar*: Come, children, and walk a little way with me, and we shall talk a while together of life and earth and Heaven. Come, Adam. *He takes Adam by the hand.* Eve? *She comes to him, enthralled, and gives him her hand.* Abel? Cain?

CAIN: Lord, there's still my corn. You haven't tasted my corn.

GOD: Oh, I can see it's all very nice. You have done quite well, Cain. Keep it up. *With which He walks into light with Adam, and Abel following behind.*

EVE, *beckoning*: Cain? *Seeing his shock*: Darling, he loved your vegetables. Come.

Cain seems to hardly hear her and takes a few dead steps following her. She goes, and he comes to a halt. Lucifer starts for him, then halts as he sees his strange expression.

LUCIFER: Now control yourself, boy. Cain?

CAIN: He never even tasted my corn.

LUCIFER: You mustn't get excited.

CAIN, *with the undercurrent of dangerous laughter*: But do you know what goes into an ear of corn! I planted twice this year; the floods washed my seeds away the first time. *His eyes fall on a flask beside the altar.* And my wine. *Going to the flask*: I was going to offer . . . *He suddenly kicks down the altar.*

LUCIFER: Listen to me—*For good measure Cain sends all the food flying with another kick.* We've got to get serious!

CAIN: Cain, serious? That's all over, Devil, now Cain starts to *live*! *He starts throwing everyone out of the shelter.*

LUCIFER: What's this, now?

CAIN: This is my house! Mine! *He faces Lucifer.* No one enters here but Cain any more. They have God, and I have this farm—and before I'm finished, my fences will stretch out to cover the earth!

LUCIFER: Adam will never agree to leave this house—

CAIN: Oh, he'll agree, all right—*he strides to his flail and brandishes it*—once I explain it to him! *He whips the flail with a whoosh, and, holding it up*: There's the only wisdom I will ever need again! *A deep hum sounds in the earth, like a dynamo.*

LUCIFER: Listen! *Cain freezes.* He has set a moaning in the earth. *Daylight changes to night; stars appear.* Look! *Both look up at the night sky.*

> He is giving you a night at noon,
> Darkening your mind to kill for him!

Frightened, Cain turns from the sky to the flail in his hand and throws it down guiltily.

> Don't let him use you. Go away. Hide yourself.

CAIN: I, hide? I was the one who thought of the offerings; from me this Sabbath came! Let them hide! I want nothing from anyone any more!

LUCIFER: But God wants a murder from you.

CAIN, *astonished*: God . . . wants . . . ?

LUCIFER: He has designed your vengeance, boy. He's boiling your blood in his hand.

CAIN: But why?

> LUCIFER: So he may stand above your crime, the
> blameless God,
> The only assurance of Mankind, and his power is safe.
> Come now,
> We'll hide you till this anger's gone.

He leads Cain a few yards; Cain moves as though being carried, staring into Lucifer's face.

ABEL'S VOICE, *calling from a distance*: Cain? Where are you? Come on!

Cain swerves about toward the voice.

LUCIFER: Don't stop!

CAIN—*a cry, as though from his bowel, to the sky*: How is Abel the favorite of God?

> LUCIFER: God has no favorites! *He grasps Cain's astounded face.* Man's a mirror to Him, Cain,
> In which He looks to see His praise.

CAIN: But I have praised Him! And Abel only played His flute!

> LUCIFER: So where is good and where is evil?
> God wants power, not morals!

ABEL'S VOICE, *closer now, calling*: Cain! We're all waiting for you!

LUCIFER, *grabbing for him*: Come!

CAIN: I have to face him first! *He breaks from Lucifer, facing in the direction of Abel's voice.*

> LUCIFER: Then face him with indifference.
> Kill love, Cain, kill whatever in you cares;
> Murder now is but another sort of praise to God!
> Don't praise Him with a death!

ABEL, *closer yet*: Cain?

> CAIN: His voice is like silver, like his life,
> And mine is the voice of the ox, the driven beast!

LUCIFER: Indifference, Cain!

Abel enters.

ABEL: Aren't you coming? God is sitting by the river, telling all about Paradise—come on! *Cain stares front.*

LUCIFER, *facing front*: I swear this, Cain—if man will not kill man, God is unnecessary! Walk away and you're free! *Cain starts to walk away.*

ABEL: Brother! God wants you there!

CAIN, *halting*: Wants *me*?

LUCIFER: Swallow it and walk!

ABEL: Of course—he loves you, Cain. He was just saying how you do everything He wants.

CAIN: Then, by God, I order you out of here and your mother and father, and never come back!

ABEL: Brother!—I've as much right here as you. *He moves toward Cain.*

CAIN: Are you even so sure of his blessing that you come to me?

ABEL: You'll not hurt me, Cain.

CAIN: Why? Am I thy servant? *He sweeps up his flail.* Am I thy fool? Run from me!

ABEL: *Astonished at the flail, he starts to back away.* Brother! God loves us both!

CAIN: You are dead to me, Abel—run!

ABEL, *halts*: I will not! Come to the Lord!

CAIN, *moving toward him, raising the flail*: Run for your life!

ABEL: Brother, let God calm you!

CAIN, *whirling about, flail raised, he calls to the air*: Save us, Lord . . . !

ABEL, *rushing to him*: Come to Him!

CAIN—*he turns on Abel, calling to God*: Now save us! *He strikes at Abel who dodges and runs.*

ABEL, *screaming*: Mother!

CAIN—*pursuing him, he strikes Abel down*: Save us! *He strikes him again on the ground.* Save us!

LUCIFER: Cain! How can you love God so!

GOD, *calling from off*: Cain! Where art thou?

Cain flings the flail away like an alien thing that somehow got into his hand. God enters rapidly, behind Him Eve and Adam.

GOD: Where is thy brother?

Cain is silent.

EVE: Where is Abel?

ADAM: Where is he?

GOD: Where is Abel, thy brother?

CAIN, *with a new, dead indifference*: I know not. Am I my brother's keeper?

GOD: The voice of thy brother's blood crieth unto me from the ground.

EVE—*seeing the corpse, like a sigh at first*: Ahhh.

ADAM, *wide-eyed*: Ohhh. *The sigh repeatedly emanating*

from her, she halts, looking down at the corpse. Adam comes and faces it. Ohhhh.

EVE—*she goes down beside the corpse, keening.* Abel? Wake, my darling!

ADAM: Abel? *Calls.* Abel!

GOD: What hast thou done!

CAIN, *with a bitter, hard grin, plus a certain intimate, familiar tone*: What had to be done. As the Lord surely knew when I laid before Him the fruit of my sweat—for which there was only Thy contempt.

GOD: But why contempt? Didn't I approve of your offering?

CAIN: As I would "approve" my ox. Abel's lamb was not "approved," it was adored, like his life!

GOD, *indignantly*: But I *like* lamb! *Cain is dumfounded.* I don't deny it, I like lamb better than onions.

LUCIFER: Surely there can be no accounting for taste.

CAIN: And this is Your justice?

GOD: Justice!

CAIN, *with a bitter laugh*: Yes, justice! Justice!

GOD: When have I ever spoken that word?

CAIN: You mean our worth and value are a question of *taste*?

GOD, *incredulously*: But Cain, there are eagles and sparrows, lions and mice—is every bird to be an eagle? Are there to be no mice? Let a man do well, and he shall be accepted.

CAIN: I have done well and I am humiliated!

GOD: You hated Abel before this day, so you cannot say you have done well.

EVE, *rising from the corpse*: You argue with *Him*? *She rushes to tear at Cain, Adam holding her back.* Kill him! He's a murderer! *Weeping, held by Adam, she calls*: Take his life!

GOD: Surely you repent this, Cain.

CAIN: When God repents His injustice, I will repent my own!

LUCIFER: Why should he repent? Who sent death down here? You did! *He points to God.* There is the murderer!

ADAM: Watch your mouth!

LUCIFER: He arranged it all from beginning to end! *Eve stops weeping, straightens, astonished, turns to God.* Do You deny Azrael was here this morning while they slept? *To Eve*: Ask him!

EVE: You sent the Angel of Death?

Pause.

GOD: Yes.

EVE: Lord God . . . did you want this?

Pause.

GOD: Eve . . . soon the multitudes will spring from this first family and cover the earth. How will the thousands be shepherded as I have shepherded thee? Only if the eye of God opens in the heart of every man; only if each himself will choose the way of life, not death. For otherwise you go as beasts, locked up in the darkness of their nature. *Slight pause.* I saw that Cain was pious, yet in him I saw envy too. And so I thought—if Cain was so enraged that he lift his hand against his brother, but then, remembering his love for Abel and for me, even in his fury lay down his arms? *To Cain:* Man!—you would have risen like a planet before the generations, the victory of God, first brother and the first to reject a murder. Oh, Cain, how I hoped for thee!

ADAM, *to Eve:* Do you understand? He was trying to help us. *She stands rigid, wide-eyed.* Eve, you must beg his pardon.

EVE, *turning to God:* But why must my child have died? You could have tested me, or Adam or Abel—we could *never* have killed.

GOD: Woman, a moment ago you commanded me to take Cain's life.

EVE: But I . . . I was *angry.*

GOD: Cain was also angry. *She turns away, rejecting.* Do you understand me? *Beginning to anger.* Then am I a wanton murderer? Speak! What am I to you?

ADAM: Eve! Tell him you understand!

EVE: I do not understand . . . why we *can't just live!*

GOD: Because without God you'll murder each other!

EVE, *furiously:* And with God? With God?

GOD: Then do you want the Devil? Tell me now before the multitudes arrive. Who do you want!

ADAM: You, Lord, you!

GOD: Why? Your innocent son is dead; why!

ADAM: Because . . . how do I know?—maybe for someone, somewhere, even this . . . is good? Right?

GOD, *outraged*: You are all worthless! The mother blames God, the father blames no one, and the son knows no blame at all. *To Lucifer*: Angel, you have won the world—and I hereby give it over to your ministry.

ADAM: *Him!*

GOD: This is the chaos you want, and him you shall have— the God who judges nothing, the God of infinite permission. I shall continue to do the hurricanes, the gorillas, and all that, but I see now that your hearts' desire is anarchy and I wash my hands. I do not want to be God . . . any more! *He starts away.*

LUCIFER, *dashing after Him*: Lord! You don't mean—not me all by myself!

GOD: That's what you've been after, isn't it?

LUCIFER: No, no—with You! It's out of the question for me to run the world alone.

GOD: But what do you need Me for?

LUCIFER: But I can't—I can't *make* anything!

GOD: Really! But you're such a superb critic.

LUCIFER: But they're two entirely different things!

GOD: Perhaps once you're in charge you'll become more creative. *He starts away again; Eve rushes to Him.*

EVE: Wait, Lord, please!

GOD: Oh, woman, for thy torment especially I am most deeply sorry. Good-bye, dear Eve. *He starts away.*

EVE: But what do we do about Cain?

Now He halts, turns, alert.

LUCIFER, *to God*: Very well, I take the world! *To Eve*: Tell him to go!

EVE, *to Lucifer*: But what about Cain?

LUCIFER: There'll be no more talk about Cain. The boy simply got caught in a rotten situation, and no emotions are called for.

GOD: She seems to have a question—

LUCIFER: She is free! She has no further questions! *To Eve*: Tell him to go back to his hurricanes.

EVE, *to Lucifer*: But he murdered my son.

GOD: But what is the question?

EVE: HE MURDERED MY SON!

GOD: And what is the *question,* woman!

LUCIFER: You've got your freedom! Stop here!

EVE, *to Lucifer*: But how—*turning to Cain's adamant face*: How do I hand him his breakfast tomorrow? How do I call him to dinner? "Come, mankiller, I have meat for thee"?

CAIN, *holding his ground, his profile to her eyes*: It was not my fault!

EVE, *crying out to God*: How can we live with him!

GOD: But what did you say to me a moment ago—"Why can't we just live?" Why can't you do it? Take your unrepentant son and start living.

LUCIFER: Why not? Will blaming Cain bring Abel back?

EVE: But shouldn't he . . . shouldn't he repent?

LUCIFER: You mean a few appropriate words will console you?

EVE: Not words, but . . . *To Cain*: Don't you feel you've done *anything*?

LUCIFER: What's the difference what he feels?

EVE, *with high anxiety*: You mean nothing has *happened*?

LUCIFER: There is no consolation, woman! Unless you want the lie of God, the false tears of a killer repenting!

EVE: But why must they be false? If he loved his brother, maybe now he feels . . . *She breaks off, backing a step from Lucifer, and turns to God*: Is this . . . why he can't be God?

GOD, *quickly*: Why can't he be God?

LUCIFER: I can and I will be—I am the truth!

EVE: But you . . . *In fear*: you don't . . .

ADAM: He doesn't love us!

EVE: Yes!

GOD: And that is why, whatever you do, it's all the same to him—it's only his power this Angel loves!

ADAM AND EVE, *rushing to God*: Father, save us!

GOD: Oh, my children, I thought you'd never understand!

LUCIFER, *with a furious, bitter irony, as God approaches the beseeching people*: And here He comes again—Father Guilt is back! *Rushing to Cain*: Cain, help me! You're the one free, guiltless man. Tell God you have no need for Him! Speak out your freedom and save the world!

CAIN—*he has been staring in silence; now he turns his dead eyes to Lucifer*: Angel, none of this seems to matter, you know? One way or the other. Why don't you let it all go?

With a near-sob Lucifer claps his hands over his ears, then, straightening, he comes to a salute before God.

LUCIFER: You have my salute! You have gorgeously pre-arranged this *entire* dialogue, and it all comes out the way You want—but You have solved absolutely nothing!

GOD: *lifting His eyes from the kneeling Adam and Eve*: Except, angel, that you will never be God. And not because I forbid, but because they will never—at least not for very long—believe it. For I made them not of dust alone, but dust and love; and by dust alone they will not, cannot long be governed. *Lucifer bursts into sobbing tears.* Why do you weep, angel? They love, and with love, kill brothers. Take heart, I see now that our war goes on.

ADAM AND EVE: No, Lord!

Lucifer looks at God now, clear-eyed, expectant.

GOD: It does go on. For love, I see, is not enough; though the Devil himself cry peace, you'll find your war. Now I want to know what is in your heart. Tell me, Man, what do you feel?

CAIN: I am thirsty.

GOD, *after a slight pause*: So in thy thirst will I sentence thee, Cain—to live. And in this loneliness shalt thou walk forever in the populous cities, a fugitive and a vagabond all the days of thy life. And whoever looks on thee will point and say, "There is the man who murdered his brother."

CAIN, *coming alive*: Better kill me now! They will stone me wherever I go!

GOD: No. I declare to all the generations: Whoever slayeth Cain, vengeance shall be taken on him sevenfold. For I will set a mark upon thee, Cain, that will keep thee from harm.

CAIN: What mark?

GOD, *holding two index fingers pointed toward Cain's face*: Come to me, my son. *Terrified, Cain comes up to His fingers, and He comes around behind Cain, who is facing front, and presses his cheeks, forming a smile which Cain cannot relax. God lowers His fingers.*

CAIN, *smiling*: What is the mark?

GOD: That smile is.

CAIN: But they will know that I killed my brother!

GOD: Yes, they will know, and you will smile forever with agony in your eyes—the sundered mark of Cain who killed for pride and power in the name of love.

Smiling, his eyes desperate, Cain turns to Eve. She cries out and hides her face in her hands. He tears at his cheeks, but his smile remains. He lowers his hands—a smiling man with astonished, terrifying eyes.

GOD: Adam? Eve? Now the way of life is revealed before you, and the way of death. Seek me only in your hearts, you will never see My face again.

Lucifer, who has been staring off, swerves about. The people come alert, startled. God turns and walks upstage.

ADAM, *rushing a half-step behind God*: What'd you say? Lord, I don't understand . . . *God continues, moving into light. Adam halts, calling.* Did you say *never*?

EVE: What does that mean? Almighty God! *She starts to run up toward Him, but He disappears among the stars. Adam, above her now, turns down to Lucifer.*

ADAM: Angel! *He comes down to Lucifer, his finger rising toward the angel.* Did he mean that you are . . . ?

Lucifer turns from the vanished God to Adam, his face twisted with puzzlement.

ADAM AND EVE, *with a heartbroken, lost cry*: Who is God?

LUCIFER: Does it really matter? Why don't you have a nice breakfast together—the three of you—and forget the whole thing? After all, whoever God is, we have to be sensible. *He walks away, glancing back to Eve.* And whenever you'd like to start the dancing—just call.

EVE: Don't ever come back!

LUCIFER, *pointing insinuatingly at her*: You know exactly what I mean.

Lucifer walks into darkness. Adam and Eve turn to Cain.

ADAM: He condemned you to wander the earth. You'll have to go.

CAIN: But he let me live; there was some forgiveness in that. There's too much work here for one man, Father.

EVE: How can you ask forgiveness? *Indicating Abel.* You can't even weep for him. You are still full of hate!

CAIN: And your hate, Mother? *She turns away.* How will I weep? You never loved Cain!

ADAM: Spare one another . . . !

EVE, *turning to the corpse*: I loved him more. *To Cain*: Yes, more than you. And God was *not* fair. To me, either. *Indicating Abel.* And I still don't understand why he had to die, or who or what rules this world. But this boy was innocent—that I know. And you killed him, and with him any claim to justice you ever had.

CAIN: I am not to blame!

EVE: Are you telling me that nothing *happened* here? I will not sit with you as though nothing happened!

ADAM: Ask her pardon! *Cain turns away from both.* Cain, we are surrounded by the beasts! And God's not coming any more—*Cain starts away.* Boy, we are all that's left responsible!—ask her pardon! *Cain, adamant, the smile fixed on his face, walks out.* Call to him. Pardon him. In God's name cry mercy, Eve, there is no other!

With his arm around her he has drawn her to the periphery, where she stands, her mouth open, struggling to speak. But she cannot, and she breaks into weeping. As though in her name, Adam calls toward the departed Cain: Mercy!

The roars, songs, and cries of the animals fill the air. Adam looks up and about, and to the world, a clear-eyed prayer: Mercy!

CURTAIN